"Anyone who knows Mack Stiles knows he would find it difficult to be boring, even if he decided to be. The book you are holding incites Christians, not least pastors, to burn to see evangelism become part of the local church's culture, a driving component of its spiritual DNA. This book is rich in practical implications, not *despite* its incessant focus on Jesus and the gospel, but precisely *because* of such focus. It deserves to be read, pondered, and implemented."

D. A. Carson, Research Professor of New Testament, Trinity Evangelical Divinity School

"The best book on evangelism would be a book that gets right to the heart of the issue and that is written by one who is himself an evangelist. In other words, it would be this book. Mack Stiles is one of the most natural, effective, determined, indefatigable evangelists that I know. I would want to know what he thinks about evangelism, whether it comes in a conversation, a letter, or an entire book. In this short volume, Mack conducts a clear and biblical exploration of how church fellowship multiplies individual evangelism. Every reader will be inspired, encouraged, and equipped to be a congregational evangelist. For the sake of the church, the gospel, and the world, this book belongs at the top of your reading list."

R. Albert Mohler, Jr., President and Joseph Emerson Brown Professor of Christian Theology, The Southern Baptist Theological Seminary

"God gifted Mack Stiles as an evangelist, and this book is the overflow of that gift. I know of few works that combine the theological rigor, pastoral wisdom, and personal experience that Mack packs into this short book. In places I was encouraged, in others challenged. I loved reading this book and recommend it heartily."

J. D. Greear, Lead Pastor, The Summit Church, Durham, North Carolina; author, *Stop Asking Jesus into Your Heart: How to Know for Sure You Are Saved*

"Mack Stiles writes about developing a culture of evangelism in a way that allows the reader to see it! We not only read the truth in this book, we drink in a vision for how our church families can live in a rich, dynamic way. This may be the shortest but most important book you ever read for the life of your church and the spread of the gospel."

Thabiti M. Anyabwile, Senior Pastor, First Baptist Church of Grand Cayman; author, *What Is a Healthy Church Member?*

"The church's ancient mission to make disciples of all nations is still our top priority today. Our need to be equipped in sharing our faith is undeniably urgent. This is a book about real people learning to share the good news about a real Messiah. It is instructive, encouraging, and compelling—you won't want to wait to apply what you learn in these pages. And if anyone knows how to equip people to speak of Jesus, it's Mack Stiles!"

> **Gloria Furman,** Pastor's wife, Redeemer Church of Dubai; mother of four; author, *Glimpses of Grace* and *Treasuring Christ When Your Hands Are Full*

"I am genuinely excited about this book. Stiles's books on evangelism are terrific because they combine practical help with theological maturity. And he actually practices what he prescribes."

> **Kevin DeYoung,** Senior Pastor, University Reformed Church, East Lansing, Michigan

"Mack Stiles has written an outstanding book not just about sharing the gospel (though it is about that) or about being a personal evangelist (though it's that, too). He's written a book about how the local church actually helps us share the gospel—eases the burden, instructs, excites, cooperates. Read this little book and be encouraged!"

> **Mark Dever,** Senior Pastor, Capitol Hill Baptist Church, Washington, D.C.; President, 9Marks

"I read this engaging book in a single sitting because I was so taken by its content and spirit. *Evangelism* is a primer on how the Bible addresses the crucial subject of sharing the gospel. I anticipate its wide and enthusiastic reception."

> **Daniel L. Akin,** President, Southeastern Baptist Theological Seminary

"I love Mack Stiles's vision of 'a culture of evangelism' permeating our churches. May God work powerfully to bring this vision to reality. This book both encourages and challenges, and, like Mack's previous books, is a great gift and blessing to God's people."

> **Randy Newman,** Teaching Fellow, C. S. Lewis Institute; author, *Questioning Evangelism, Corner Conversations*, and *Bringing the Gospel Home*

"Plenty of books discuss individual evangelism. This one, however, zeroes in on an entire culture. Not methods or programs, but an ethos. Spread this book through your church and see what happens."

John Folmar, Senior Pastor, The United Church of Dubai

"This is a Christ-exalting, gospel-saturated book on evangelism unlike any other. Rather than giving you a *personal* methodology, it deeply motivates you to proclaim and bear the fruit of the revolutionary news of Jesus *as a church body*. And what makes it even more valuable is that I have seen Mack Stiles model the attitudinal culture he writes about on several continents to the glory of God. He is the most gifted evangelist I have seen God use (so far), bar none. *Evangelism* is a must read for every pastor *and* church member."

Richard Chin, National Director, Australian Fellowship of Evangelical Students; South Pacific Regional Secretary, International Fellowship of Evangelical Students

"It did not take long for this book to become my favorite book on evangelism—in part because I could not put it down! The gospel is so clear and the help I received is so tangible. But let the reader count the cost. It may stir something within you that you cannot shake. I will now never be satisfied with anything less than cultivating a culture of evangelism in the church I pastor. I praise God for what he gave me through this book and I pray for more."

Jason C. Meyer, Pastor for Preaching and Vision, Bethlehem Baptist Church

"Imagine a local church where every member knows the gospel and walks in step with it, where all are concerned for unbelieving people, where it is natural for leaders and members to talk about evangelistic opportunities, and where members are regularly inviting unbelievers to read the Bible together or to attend small group Bible studies or Sunday services. If that sounds encouraging to you, then you'll want to read this book and let Mack guide you step by step toward a culture of evangelism where evangelism is simply a natural outflow of the gospel life."

Juan R. Sanchez, Jr., Pastor, High Pointe Baptist Church, Austin, Texas

9Marks: Building Healthy Churches

Edited by Mark Dever and Jonathan Leeman

Expositional Preaching: How We Speak God's Word Today, David Helm

Sound Doctrine: How a Church Grows in the Love and Holiness of God, Bobby Jamieson

The Gospel: How the Church Portrays the Beauty of Christ, Ray Ortlund

Evangelism: How the Whole Church Speaks of Jesus, J. Mack Stiles

Church Membership: How the World Knows Who Represents Jesus, Jonathan Leeman

Church Discipline: How the Church Protects the Name of Jesus, Jonathan Leeman

Discipling: How to Help Others Follow Jesus, Mark Dever

Church Elders: How to Shepherd God's People Like Jesus, Jeramie Rinne

Conversion: How God Creates a People, Michael Lawrence

Missions: How the Local Church Goes Global, Andy Johnson

Biblical Theology: How the Church Faithfully Teaches the Gospel, Nick Roark and Robert Cline

Prayer: How Praying Together Shapes the Church, John Onwuchekwa

BUILDING HEALTHY CHURCHES

EVANGELISM

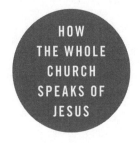

HOW
THE WHOLE
CHURCH
SPEAKS OF
JESUS

J. MACK STILES

Foreword by David Platt

WHEATON, ILLINOIS

Hardcover ISBN: 978-1-4335-4465-1
ePub ISBN: 978-1-4335-4468-2
PDF ISBN: 978-1-4335-4466-8
Mobipocket ISBN: 978-1-4335-4467-5

Library of Congress Cataloging-in-Publication Data

Stiles, J. Mack, 1956-
   Evangelism : how the whole church speaks of Jesus / Mack Stiles.
      pages cm. — (9Marks: building healthy churches)
   Includes bibliographical references and index.
   ISBN 978-1-4335-4465-1 (hc)
   1. Witness bearing (Christianity) 2. Evangelistic work. 3. Missions. I. Title.
BV4520.S6747   2014
269'.2—dc23   2013038258

Crossway is a publishing ministry of Good News Publishers.

LB		30	29	28	27	26	25	24	23	22	21	20
21	20	19	18	17	16	15	14	13	12	11	10	9

To my children: Tristan, David, Isaac, and Stephanie
Psalm 127:3–5

CONTENTS

SERIES PREFACE

The 9Marks series of books is premised on two basic ideas. First, the local church is far more important to the Christian life than many Christians today perhaps realize.

Second, local churches grow in life and vitality as they organize their lives around God's Word. God speaks. Churches should listen and follow. It's that simple. When a church listens and follows, it begins to look like the One it is following. It reflects his love and holiness. It displays his glory. A church will look like him as it listens to him.

So our basic message to churches is, don't look to the best business practices or the latest styles; look to God. Start by listening to God's Word again.

Out of this overall project comes the 9Marks series of books. Some target pastors. Some target church members. Hopefully all will combine careful biblical examination, theological reflection, cultural consideration, corporate application, and even a bit of individual exhortation. The best Christian books are always both theological and practical.

It's our prayer that God will use this volume and the others to help prepare his bride, the church, with radiance and splendor for the day of his coming.

FOREWORD

I remember the first time I met Mack Stiles. We were speaking at a conference together in the United States, and while I and other conference speakers spent most of our time talking with each other, Mack was rarely to be found among us. I wondered why not, until I discovered that Mack was spending most of his time talking about Jesus with the people who worked behind the scenes at the facility where the conference was being held. From that first interaction with this brother, I knew I had much to learn from him.

Not long thereafter, I had the privilege of being overseas in the location where Mack leads a ministry to college students and serves as one of the elders of a church. I was preaching at the church one morning, and after I finished, Mack started introducing me to all sorts of people. Here's the general gist of how those conversations went (though I've changed the names).

"Hi, my name is Abdul," one man said to me. "I grew up as a Muslim, but a couple of years ago, God graciously saved me from my sins and myself through Christ."

"That's wonderful," I responded. "How did you hear the gospel?"

"Through my friendship with Mack," Abdul said. "He asked me one day if I wanted to read through the Gospel of Mark with

13

him. I told him I was willing, and within a few months, the Holy Spirit had opened my heart to believe."

Then I turned to another man, who introduced himself. "Hey, I'm Rajesh. I was a Hindu all my life until someone invited me to this church. I didn't know anything about Christianity until I got here, but Mack and others started meeting with me and showing me who Christ is and what Christ has done. I was overwhelmed, and after exploring all sorts of questions that I had with Mack, I trusted in Christ for my salvation."

Behind Abdul and Rajesh was Matthew. Matthew said to me: "I grew up a nominal Christian devoid of any relationship with Christ, but last year God opened my eyes to what faith in Christ truly means. I repented of my sins and believed in him."

"Let me guess," I said. "Mack led you to Christ, right?"

"No," Matthew said. "Abdul and Rajesh did. They spent hours with me in Scripture, showing me what it means to follow Christ." Then Matthew asked me: "Can I introduce you to Stephen? He's a friend of mine who is exploring Christianity right now, and he came with me to the church gathering this morning."

These conversations went on and on with person after person. I stood literally amazed by the grace of God, not just upon one Christian passionate about sharing the gospel, but upon an entire community passionate about sharing the gospel. As I looked around, I observed a contagious culture of evangelism across the church. It is a culture of evangelism that is not ultimately dependent on events, projects, programs, and ministry professionals. Instead, it is a culture of evangelism that is built on people filled with the power of God's Spirit proclaiming the gospel of God's grace in the context of their everyday lives and relationships.

As a result, I truly cannot think of anyone better to write a book not just on cultivating the discipline of evangelism as a Christian, but on creating a culture of evangelism in the church. When I read through this book, I found myself high-lighting sentence after sentence, paragraph after paragraph, praying all along about the way the Lord might use me to create such a culture of evangelism in the church I pastor.

This book is biblical and practical. It's good for church members and leaders, and ultimately it's glorifying to God. May the Lord see fit to bless it in your life and church—and in multitudes of lives and churches—to the end that his church might see more and more Abduls, Rajeshes, Matthews, and Stephens come to saving faith in Christ here and around the world.

David Platt
Senior pastor, The Church at Brook Hills
Birmingham, Alabama

INTRODUCTION

"And what is your book about, dear?"

So asked the elderly woman who was picking up my mother-in-law for their weekly game of bridge. As I put the walker in the back seat of her car, I pondered what to say. I wanted to say, "It's not just a book on evangelism, but a book on developing a culture of evangelism." She sensed my hesitation, glanced at my mother-in-law, and said, "Well, what is the title, dear?"

Again I paused, looking up at the sky. My mother-in-law came to the rescue: "It's about evangelism." She said this in that tone reserved for people whose hearing is not quite what it used to be.

"Oh," said her friend. There was a bit of a question mark after her "oh." I shut the car door.

"Well, it's more about getting the *whole church* to share their faith," I said.

The friend looked even more puzzled. "Hmm," she said. Then she turned to my mother-in-law. "Well, Ann, I know you're *so* proud," she said as she patted my arm. Never mind that the author himself couldn't seem to figure out what his book was about.

Let me try to do better for you. This book is about *biblical* evangelism. Now I don't think that Christian people set out to write books on evangelism based on unbiblical principles. But it happens. It happens because there are wrong ideas about the critical components of evangelism. Usually the wrong ideas are based on marketing principles or on human understandings about how to argue someone into the kingdom. If we don't have biblical evangelism nailed down, we may not be doing evangelism.

For example, a housewife meeting with a friend over coffee may be evangelizing, while a brilliant Christian apologist speaking to thousands in a church sanctuary may not be. Few see it that way, but that's because we have false understandings of what evangelism is. Defending the faith is a fine thing to do, but it is easy to give apologetics for Christianity without explaining the gospel—and we cannot evangelize without the gospel.

We need to know what we're talking about when we say "evangelism," "conversion," or even "gospel." Those words raise different definitions in people's minds and often come with question marks. If Christians don't understand those basic concepts, we will quickly spin out of the biblical orbit. So we'll spend some time wrestling with definitions in chapter 1.

By the way, many might want to use the word *missional* for what I am calling a "culture of evangelism." I understand why they might, but I want to retain the word *evangelism*. It's an important biblical word, and that's the word I use throughout the book.

This book *is* about evangelism, but more than that, it's also about developing a culture of evangelism. That's chapter 2. When I say "a culture of evangelism," I don't mean lots of programs for evangelism. In fact, it may surprise you that I would encourage many churches to cut their evangelistic programs. I'll tell you why later, but it's enough to say here that I want to explore how we can integrate the responsibility that every Christian bears to share the faith into the life of our church fellowships, multiplying individual efforts.

Much of our problem with evangelism is that we don't have a big enough view of the church. I believe that God loves the world and has a wonderful plan for evangelism: his church. That is chapter 3.

Since this book is about evangelism and a culture of evangelism in church life, it also describes the platforms—often neglected—that Christians must build for healthy evangelistic efforts. This is the topic of chapter 4. Examples:

- Intentional evangelism preparation
- A gospel-shaped way of life
- Not assuming the gospel
- Evangelism as a spiritual discipline
- Prayer
- Evangelistic leadership

Then, of course, we need to explore basic principles that shape the actual practice of sharing our faith, those things we need to do to live as Christ's ambassadors to a sin-sick world. That's chapter 5.

I have good friends who think of me as an evangelist; I'm not so sure. I do long for people to know Jesus. And I feel as though I am someone seeking to be faithful in evangelism. But I want people to know that I really face fears of what others think of me when I talk about spiritual issues. I'm very aware of my failings and limitations in evangelism. And looking around, I see many others who are much better evangelists than I. If I'm an evangelist, I'm a mediocre one.

But there is one thing that I think, by God's grace, I am good at: I believe God has used me to develop cultures of evangelism. Over the years, as I've helped to establish student ministries or plant churches, I've wanted to make sure that those communities had evangelism in their DNA, as their ethos and culture.

That is a driving passion for me, and that's why I'm excited about this book. It's a way to take those things I've loved putting together and share them with you.

1

OF ALTAR CALLS AND LASER LIGHTS

I was a freshly minted 1970s-era Jesus freak. During the first months of my first year in college, I led my friend and room-mate, John, to Jesus. One Sunday, not long after, we decided to attend the large Baptist church in downtown Memphis.

I cut quite a figure: I sported a huge red Afro, bell-bottom jeans, and a purple wool trench coat. We were amid crew cuts and suits.

The preacher preached, all stanzas were sung, and then came the invitation. The preacher announced sternly that he would rather have someone leave during his sermon than during the invitation, "the most important part of the service."

The appeal came for people to give their lives to Jesus. Hands were raised. We were thanked and then told to "just slip out" of our seats and come forward. "If you can't publicly stand up for Jesus in church, you won't ever stand up for him outside these walls," the preacher said. The logic seemed ironclad to me.

John, whose head was bowed but whose eyes were opened (against instructions), whispered to me, "Do you think I should go forward?"

"Well, it can't hurt," I whispered back, "I'll go with you." John popped up from the pew and I followed.

Dozens "slipped" out of their seats and streamed forward. Unbeknownst to us, they were mostly ushers. Up front, the semicircular rows of pews surrounded us. The congregation, more numerous than had appeared from our back-row seats, seemed to lean forward and focus on us, smiling.

In a flash, the preacher was by my side. "Son," he said to me in a kindly voice, "why are you here today?" He held his mike down against his leg and curled the long speaker cord behind his feet with a practiced flick of the wrist.

"Well," I said, "my friend John here accepted Jesus a couple of weeks ago, and he wanted to stand up for Jesus." The pastor glanced over at John, whose life was a mess, but who dressed conservatively. He nodded to John, "That's wonderful, son." Turning back to me, he said, "And what brings you forward?"

I was gazing up at the balcony and the bright Klieg lights with a sort of gee-whiz, country-boy-in-the-big-city look on my face. "Well, I . . . wanted to support John," I stammered.

"I see," he said, nodding, his arm now draped over my shoulder. "Are you a Christian, son?"

"I am," I said.

"And would you like to rededicate your life to Jesus?" The theological complexities of this question escaped me, so I said, "Well, sure, I guess."

The preacher then pressed the microphone to his lips and stared up at the balcony, too. He located the recently installed TV camera and pointed to it with his hand, fingers spread. "I'd like to say to all you in TV land, these two young men have

22

come to give their lives to Jesus. You can do that in your home, right now, where you sit . . ."

It took me years to figure out what had just happened.

WHAT IS EVANGELISM?

When I think back to that service so many years ago, I want to ask: Did evangelism happen that morning in that church?

We should be careful how we answer. Many people have become Christians when they walked an aisle after hearing an altar call. Recently, at a pastor's convention at Southeastern Seminary, the president, Danny Akin, noted that the gathered pastors were culturally sophisticated, well educated, and theologically robust. None of them would think of leading an altar call such as the one I experienced in Memphis. But then Akin asked, "How many of you came to faith in a church that evangelized in ways you would now reject?" Almost every pastor raised his hand.

This response should give us pause. There is much room for humility when it comes to evangelism. We need to acknowledge that God is sovereign and can do as he wills to bring people to himself. There is no formula that dictates how God must work in evangelism. And though we may disagree with the evangelistic practices of individuals, ministries, or churches, we must also recognize that when people develop good-hearted commitments to evangelism, God can produce true fruit.

I, for one, will take people practicing evangelism as best they can over those who forgo evangelism until they have the perfect practice. Remember how gently Priscilla and Aquila instructed Apollos in his evangelistic efforts (Acts 18:26)? Paul even rejoiced over selfishly motivated evangelism that caused trouble for him (Phil. 1:17–18). So when people come to faith through strange means and methods, we should first take heart that God can take the smallest seeds of gospel truth and grow them into the great fruit of gospel reconciliation in people's hearts.

Let me be clear: I do not think altar calls are catagorically wrong. Yet when I think back to my experience in Memphis, it's easy to see how the methods of those days were driven mostly by a desire for instant results: there was too much emphasis on a decision or on walking an aisle, too much concern about the watching TV audience, and too little concern about the actual state of my soul and my sin.

Many people have responded to altar calls over the decades. But for all who have been genuinely converted when they responded, there have been many more who merely came to the front of a church building out of some other compulsion—just like John and me. Most important, even though people come to Jesus through various means, the Bible *never* uses results to guide or justify evangelistic practice.

So when we set out to practice evangelism, we must start with biblical foundations. We must look to these to shape, guard, and inform how we share our faith rather than starting by looking for a way to gain maximum impact. We must be very careful to conform our evangelistic practice to the Bible, because this honors God.

Sadly, what often informs our evangelistic practices is the world—perhaps the business world or the self-help section in the bookstore—rather than the Scriptures. Satan plays to our desire for results by offering a bigger TV ministry or financial profit. He even tempts us with seemingly good-hearted desires such as an expanded membership or the undying belief that if a child prays a sinner's prayer, he or she has become a committed believer regardless of how he or she lives. In all this, people trade biblical principles for worldly desires, and our evangelistic practices get twisted.

Paul could rejoice over the gospel being preached regardless of motive because he knew God would accomplish his purposes through his Word. But Paul also corrected twisted evangelistic practices: he stressed that we must not manipulate, change the message, or deceive (e.g., 2 Cor. 4:1–2). Instead, we should seek pure motives in love for people and Christ, with a deep conviction of truth (2 Cor. 5:11–15). And we must trust that the Lord will add to our numbers (Acts 2:47).

Think of how much in that Memphis church service teetered on the edge of error:

- Did the pastor truly believe that the most important part of the service was the invitation rather than the Word of God rightly preached?
- Where in the Bible do we see people raising their hands to ask Jesus into their hearts? And when did walking an aisle replace baptism as a public display of our faith—at a *Baptist* church, for crying out loud?
- Wasn't it manipulative to have ushers slip out of their seats in an apparent response to the invitation? Didn't the use of unbiblical terms such as "rededicate your life to Jesus" fail to put forth the truth plainly (2 Cor. 4:2)?

- Did the pastor mean to publicly lie when he said John and I had just given our lives to Jesus, though we really had not? Or was he so blinded by cultural lenses that he just missed the two brothers in Christ who stood before him? Were we just a foil to show the world the effectiveness of his evangelistic efforts?

Actually, the two guys standing before him were the biggest thing he missed, and that oversight is what makes me want to jump up and down and holler. He missed a living example of the best kind of evangelism: an eighteen-year-old kid who could not have found the book of Mark without help from the table of contents had just led his friend to Jesus simply by loving him enough to explain what he knew about the gospel message. And I suspect that the congregation was so blinded by the razzmatazz of a slick program and a TV audience that they didn't think about it, either.

A DEFINITION FOR EVANGELISM

So how do we know when evangelism is happening? Well, the answer depends on how we define evangelism. Defining evangelism in a biblical way helps us align our evangelistic practice with the Scriptures. Here's a definition that has served me well for many years:

Evangelism is teaching the gospel with the aim to persuade.

Sort of dinky, huh? I bet most people would expect much more from such an important theological word. But this definition, small as it is, offers a far better balance in which to weigh our evangelistic practice than looking at how many people have responded to an appeal.

Around the same time that John and I attended the Memphis church, I bought John a Bible. It was the Amplified Bible, which, if you haven't seen it, offers stacks of synonyms for key words. Here is how the Amplified Bible might have expanded my definition:

> Evangelism is teaching (heralding, proclaiming, preaching) the gospel (the message from God that leads us to salvation) with the aim (hope, desire, goal) to persuade (convince, convert).

Notice that the definition does not require an immediate outward response. Walking an aisle, raising a hand, or even praying a prayer may tell us that evangelism has happened, but such actions are not what evangelism is. Notice, too, that if any of the four components are missing, we are probably doing something other than evangelism.

If I could, I would love to go back in time and teach the church in Memphis what evangelism really is. I would warn that there is much sickness in the church worldwide because of churches calling something evangelism when it is not. "Please," I would beg, "when you teach, don't teach people about how to behave during an invitation. Teach clearly what the gospel is and what is required of a person to turn to Christ."

I would urge the church to aim to persuade, but to persuade without manipulation. I would encourage them not to exclude what is hard about the Christian life, however tempting that may be; not to confuse human response for a move of the Spirit; and not to lie about results. "And please," I would say, "be wary of calling people Christians without some evidence that they are truly converted followers."

Of course, by today's standards, it's easy to sneer at those old church practices. But if we are honest, we have to say that we face the same temptation to sacrifice biblical principles for results and "success." As I look around, I don't see that much has changed besides the form in which we practice unbiblical evangelism. The gospel often remains untaught, and unbiblical words water down the poignant true meaning of sin, death, and hell, or confuse those who are genuinely seeking truth.

Promises of health and wealth deceive the most vulnerable: the poor, disadvantaged, and sick. And many churches offer a costless, comfortable, and benefit-giving "gospel" that is found nowhere in the Scriptures. In fact, the gospel is subverted with what Paul calls "different gospels," which are not gospels at all (Gal. 1:6–7). By catering to the desires of people, churches communicate that their focus is on non-Christians, not on the glory of God displayed by his people worshiping him.

The soaring choir riffs have been replaced by laser light shows, so that a church service becomes an avenue for entertainment rather than worship. Jesus was engaging, but he never entertained; there is a huge difference, one that is lost on the modern church. Likewise, appealing for friends, followers, and converts through social media seems much like yesteryear's TV camera in the balcony: both can tempt church leaders to miss the people in front of them. The high-pressure sales job has been replaced by the soft sell of self-help.

These kinds of things are the result of the same worldly temptations that undermine biblical evangelism, so much so that those who sneer at the old practices may need to apologize to that church back in Memphis.

But there is an answer to such temptations. It's no different today than it was in my first year in college or in the first churches in Paul's day. The solution is to fix biblically principled, gospel-centered evangelism in our minds and hearts. It is to learn how to teach the gospel with integrity and to keep the big-picture aim of true conversion in view.

So let's carefully "amplify" the four parts of my definition: "teaching," "gospel," "aim," and "persuade."

TEACHING

First, there is no evangelism without words. After all, Jesus is the Word, and the Word was with God (John 1:1).

The most important use of words in evangelism is teaching. If you think about it, this makes rational sense. We humans are unable to figure out a way of salvation on our own. Therefore, salvation must be revealed to us by God through his words.

Teaching is also the pattern of the Bible. The Bible is a book of teaching. From Genesis to Revelation, the Bible teaches us. And the Bible tells us to teach others: our kids, our neighbors, the foreigners in our midst. Older women are instructed to teach younger women. The only qualification for elders, besides being careful followers of Jesus, is that they are able to teach.

Perhaps because teaching is everywhere in the Scriptures,

we can miss its significance. Jesus saw that the crowds were like sheep without a shepherd, so he fed thousands with a few loaves of bread and fish (Mark 6:34–44; Luke 9:10–17). These miracles amaze us, as they should. But the interesting thing is that in each instance, Jesus's *first* act of compassion was to teach.

Many of us think of preaching when we think of evangelism, as we should. I, for one, want any sermon I give to contain the gospel. Certainly Paul did his share of evangelistic preaching. But often when Paul describes his ministry, he says it is a teaching ministry (1 Tim. 2:7; 2 Tim. 1:11). J. I. Packer, in his survey of Paul's evangelistic practice, says that Paul's method of evangelism was primarily a teaching method.[1]

This is good news for those of us who don't get to preach every Sunday. Not all of us can be preachers, but we can all teach the gospel as opportunity comes. I often wonder whether more people come to faith over lunch when someone asks, "What did you think about the sermon today?" than during the sermon itself. Great things happen when we can teach the gospel.

Being able to teach the gospel benefits our spiritual lives as it makes sure we are living according to gospel themes. One of the first things we ought to do at the Communion table is to check whether our lives are aligned with the gospel. Ask yourself: Am I living a life of faith in Christ's work? Am I applying gospel grace to those around me? Do I give sacrificial forgiveness to those who have wronged me?

If you do not know how to teach the gospel, you may not truly understand it. And if you do not understand it, you may not be a true Christian. I know many people who thought they were believers, but when they began to study the gospel in order to teach it, they realized they had never truly repented of sin and put their faith in Jesus.

But most important, remember that the gospel must be taught before someone can become a Christian.

When I have led people to Christ over the years, it has usually been because a non-Christian was willing to study the Scriptures with me. Perhaps it was a group of students looking into the Gospel of Mark at a camp or conference. It could have been a couple of people in a coffee shop or just one person during a lunch break. No matter where or with whom, the process is simple: we read the passage and talk about what it means. Over time, in ones and twos, people come to Jesus because they are taught the gospel. Such teaching may not be as exciting as a massive revival, but if every Christian did this with non-Christian friends, it would have far greater reach and authenticity.

GOSPEL

We don't teach math or biology. We teach the gospel. It's important to teach the gospel well because there is much confusion about it around the world.

There are two mistakes we can make about the gospel. We can make it too small or too big. Both mistakes turn on a very small hinge: misunderstandings about implications of the gospel. These implications flow out of our belief in the gospel message.

A Shrunken Gospel

We make the gospel too small by thinking it only "gets us saved," that it is a sort of fire insurance, without understanding that it has implications for all of life.

Since the gospel manifests the heart of God, it makes sense that the themes of the gospel should inform how we live—themes such as love, reconciliation, forgiveness, faith, humility, repentance, and more. Then we see that the gospel becomes both the door of salvation and the pattern for life.

Tim Keller has written wonderfully about gospel-centered living, how the gospel is not merely the ABCs of the Christian life—the way of salvation—but the A to Z of the Christian life.[2] It informs the way we live life. We will talk more about the gospel-centered life in chapter 4.

A Bloated Gospel

We make the gospel too big when we say that the gospel is everything. We do this when we think that we are saved by faith *and* the gospel's various implications. For example, much of the Christian world believes we are saved by faith and good deeds. Others, maybe the majority, believe that it is faith and the law.

Many things have been added to the gospel throughout history. It is always the same mistake. People add things that may be good, even religious, such as living a moral life, taking care of the poor, or seeing the sacraments of baptism and Communion as critical for salvation. All of these are important parts of the Christian life and privileges for Christians. But while they spring out of the gospel, they cannot save us.

Additions to the gospel, however good or good-hearted, corrupt the gospel.

A Good Definition of the Gospel

So when we talk about living the life of a Christian, we are talking about living out the themes and implications of the gospel. But when we talk about salvation, we focus on the gospel message. When we share our faith, we center on that *message* that leads to salvation. It's important to note that when the Bible uses the word *gospel*, in the Old Testament[3] as well as the New, it always does so in relationship to salvation.

Here's a good working definition:

> The gospel is the joyful message from God that leads us to salvation.

This is another definition that appears to be underwhelming because we must ask, "What, then, is the message of salvation?"

The gospel *message* answers four big questions: Who is God? Why are we in such a mess? What did Christ do? And how can we get back to God? There are no more important questions to deal with in the world, and the answers are summarized in this outline: God, Man, Christ, Response (see the appendix for various Scripture passages that support this outline):

- God is our Creator. He is loving, holy, and just. One day he will execute perfect justice against all sin.
- People are made in the image of God. We are beautiful and amazing creatures with dignity, worth, and value. But

33

through our willful, sinful rebellion against God, we have turned from being his children to his enemies. Still, all people have the capacity to be in a restored loving relationship with the living God.

- Christ is the Son of God, whose sinless life gave him the ability to become the perfect sacrifice. Through his death on the cross, he ransomed sinful people. Christ's death paid for the sins of all who come to him in faith. Christ's resurrection from the dead is the ultimate vindication of the truth of these claims.
- The response God requires from us is to acknowledge our sin, repent, and believe in Christ. So we turn from sin, especially the sin of unbelief, and turn to God in faith, with the understanding that we will follow him the rest of our days.

Another way to tell the same story is in an outline of Creation, Fall, Redemption, and Consummation. There are many other good summaries of the gospel. The particular outline you use doesn't matter as long as you teach the message people must know to be reconciled with God.

The hope in evangelism is that we so steep ourselves in gospel truth and gospel living, and so apply ourselves to gospel study, that the gospel can't help but come out of us.

AIM

As we teach the gospel, we have an aim. *Aim* is a small word, and it might be easy to skip over it as we parse the definition of evangelism. But aim may be the thing that trips us up most often in evangelism, especially more mature Christians.

Our aim springs from understanding that everyone we talk to is headed to one of two ends: eternal life or eternal punishment. So we don't just lay out gospel facts academically or haphazardly. We have an aim or direction in our gospel teaching.

Aim also reminds us that people need more than a data transfer. Some who think of evangelism as only teaching do a good job of explaining, expanding, and answering questions, as we all should. All Christians should apply themselves to think through reasons for the hope we have in Christ, reasons that sweep aside the objections and questions. But as we set out the facts of the gospel, remembering evangelism's aim helps us to be compassionate, understanding, and loving (1 Pet. 3:15).

Having an aim helps us keep perspective on what we're doing. It steers us toward an end. Our aim helps us remember that much is at stake: to see people moved from darkness to light, from bondage to freedom. Aiming for something bigger helps us know which fights to pick and which to avoid.

I was on a radio show when a woman called: "Should I go to a Catholic christening for my sister's baby boy?" she asked. Then she began unloading some anger, even hatred, over the fact that her sister thought this would "save" her baby.

I interrupted: "I think you should go, but not to support an unbiblical understanding of conversion. I think you should go because you are shooting for a bigger target than just correcting your sister's theological misunderstanding about christening. You should go and be supportive, filled with love, because you long to have a voice to speak into your sister's life with the only way that she can be saved . . . and into your nephew's life down the road, for that matter."

I wanted her to have a better aim so she wouldn't miss the target of evangelism.

PERSUADE

In evangelism, not just any aim will do. There is a very specific bull's-eye to our aim: to persuade people to convert, to become followers of Jesus.

Paul says we persuade others to follow Jesus (2 Cor. 5:11). I find the word *persuade* helpful, as it guards us from error: we persuade, but we do not manipulate; we persuade, but we are not the ones who bring about repentance or conversion. Of course, we long to see people converted because we understand that conversion is required for them to become Christians. But true conversion is the work of the Holy Spirit.

Conversion is actually the point of Christian faith that is most often misunderstood. It was confusing when Jesus taught it to a religious leader of his day (John 3). It is confusing to Christians and non-Christians today. So it's good to spend some time explaining it.

In the Muslim context where I live, many people from other faith backgrounds find it disorienting to hear me preach that no one is born a Christian, that all Christians are converts. Even those from Christian backgrounds are confused about conversion, because many come from traditions that emphasize that a person is a Christian because of external reasons. But the Bible clearly teaches that conversion is not a function of your parents' religion, of which church you join, or of what your passport says. It's not based on your academic achievements, even if they are from a religious institution. Conversion comes from true, conscious, genuine faith in Jesus.

But just as we cannot produce conversion, neither can we produce genuine faith. This also is the Holy Spirit's territory.

My friend Jeff was speaking to his fellow stockbroker about Christianity over lunch. As the conversation wound down, Jeff's colleague said with a patronizing tone, "Yeah, Jeff, I just wish I had your faith."

Jeff responded: "Well, faith is a gift. It really doesn't have anything to do with me. God is the one who gives it, so I'll pray for the gift of faith for you." This was not the answer the man expected, but it was exactly right. Conversion is required, but conversion is a function of genuine faith, which is given by the Spirit.

But perhaps the most important thing to understand about conversion is what it looks like after it happens.

FIRE IN A SYNAGOGUE: WHAT THE TRULY CONVERTED LOOK LIKE

Conversion isn't merely a good feeling. It's not just a change of mind. It's not turning over a new leaf. Those things may happen, but they can happen for reasons other than conversion. True conversion is unique. It's born out of repentance and faith, and its fruit is a changed life.

Recently, I went to hear James McPherson, the Pulitzer Prize-winning historian, lecture on naval battles during the Civil War. The lecture, sponsored by the local historical society, was held in a large synagogue. The auditorium was packed. There was a certain electricity in the air as we waited to hear from the well-known professor from Princeton.

As Dr. McPherson took the stage, he also took command.

His resonant voice, dry wit, and astounding command of the material captivated the audience. But midway through the lecture, the fire alarm sounded. This was a serious alarm. There wasn't merely a loud "blat blat blat" coming from electronic horns; there were also strobe lights that ticked blinding flashes at odd intervals.

Dr. McPherson froze. His wide-eyed look reminded me of an owl woken suddenly from slumber. He rotated his head from side to side, not knowing what to do. Since no one in the audience apparently attended the synagogue, no one took charge. We just looked around, smiling at our neighbors and wondering what to do. For what seemed like an eternity, the alarm continued. People in the chairs began talking in small groups while waiting for the alarm to go off.

"Maybe there really is a fire," I thought. But I quickly dismissed the idea: false alarms are the norm; I figured the alarm just needed to be reset. Besides, no one else seemed to think there was a problem—except for one man who stood up, calmly walked to the exit, and left the building. I'm not sure that many noticed him. Soon the alarm stopped and Dr. McPherson continued where he had left off.

If this is a parable of true conversion, there was only one convert in the room, only one true believer; the rest of us were stuck in our rationalization. Some might have thought there was a fire, but they didn't really believe it enough to walk out. We aren't persuaded in a biblical sense unless we repent, place genuine faith in Jesus, and walk with him.

There you have it: the four parts of my definition of evangelism.

WHAT HAPPENS IF WE GET EVANGELISM WRONG?

Evangelism is teaching the gospel (the message from God that leads us to salvation) with the aim to persuade. If a church does not understand biblical evangelism, over time that church will be subverted. If we don't practice healthy evangelism, the dominoes start to fall:

- The focus of preaching and teaching turns to living a moral life, not a gospel-centered life.
- Non-Christians are lulled into thinking that they are okay in their lost state.
- Christians think that non-Christians are believers because they made a superficial outward commitment.
- The church baptizes those who are not believers.
- The church allows non-Christians into membership.
- Eventually, non-Christians become leaders in the church.
- A church becomes a subculture of nominalism.

Unbiblical evangelism is a method of assisted suicide for a church, so there is much at stake in getting evangelism right.

Evangelists are like the trained counselors who are called upon to talk to people threatening suicide. Their aim is to talk potential jumpers off "the ledge." The counselors don't use force and don't lie. They use truth, hope, and reason to persuade. They stay calm and cool; plus, they are kind, because they know a life is at stake.

Just like them, we use the hope of the gospel to reason. We keep our cool and are kind, too, because we remember what is at stake. Our aim is to persuade people off the ledge. And there is great relief when someone *is* persuaded and moves into the safe embrace of the Savior.

2

A CULTURE OF EVANGELISM

In his letter to the Philippians, the apostle Paul wrote:

> I hold you in my heart, for you are all partakers with me of grace, both in my imprisonment and in the defense and confirmation of the gospel. For God is my witness, how I yearn for you all with the affection of Christ Jesus. (Phil. 1:7–8)

I identify strongly with Paul's affection for his friends in Philippi. For as long as I can remember, I've lived with friends.

I brought friends home with me as a kid. My earliest memories are of our backyard filled with friends—to the delight of my outgoing mother.

In university, I rarely studied alone—well, okay, I rarely studied, but when I did, it was with a band of brothers and sisters.

I married my best friend.

On the job, I most enjoy work that puts me with people I admire and call friends.

I've taken friends with me to live on different continents around the world and made friends with the people who lived there, too.

There are struggles, of course. I'm struggling (unsuccessfully) to figure out how to write a book with friends, for instance. But despite the occasional required individual activity, my life's desire, from the backyard to the far reaches of the world, is to be with friends. I have always had this desire; it's how I'm wired.

So why does an extrovert, like me, think of evangelism only in individual terms? Maybe it's because almost all instruction I've ever heard about evangelism has been about personal evangelism. Even the teaching I've done over the years has mostly been about personal evangelism. That's odd to me, especially because evangelism is scary and I don't like doing scary things by myself. I bet you don't either.

Sure, there is that rare person who is uninhibited about sharing the faith. But if you ask most normal people what hinders their evangelism, the vast majority will tell you it's fear: fear of rejection, of looking stupid, or of being lumped into weird stereotypes about evangelists. With apologies to G. K. Chesterton, it's not that evangelism has been tried and found wanting, it's that evangelism has been found difficult and left untried.

So why do something scary and difficult by yourself? Believers, band together! Evangelize with believing friends who will pull you along.

I appreciate personal evangelism, and we need to be equipped for it. But since I believe in the church as the engine of evangelism, we need to develop cultures of evangelism in our local churches, too. We want whole churches that speak of Jesus.

Think of the benefits of communal evangelism:

- We hold one another accountable.
- We strengthen our mutual resolve.
- We learn from one another.
- We rejoice together in success and cry together in failure.
- We bond through shared experiences in intense situations.

It just makes sense to share our faith alongside friends.

Actually, it doesn't take much effort to convince most Christians that evangelism with community is the way to go. It's not even hard to find people pulling together to accomplish an evangelistic task.

But usually when we think of evangelism in community, we think of evangelistic programs, which is not the same. By "program," I mean the occasional big event with a well-known speaker or exciting topic. At some point during the event, there is a presentation of the gospel. Or maybe the program is low-key, geared for seekers, such as a service project or a sports program, with the hope that it might open a door for a spiritual conversation.

God can use programs. I know people who have come to faith at evangelistic events. For the record, I often promote and speak at evangelistic programs. But I don't think programs are the most effective, or even the primary, way we should do evangelism.

AN EASTER PAGEANT PROGRAM

A church in my hometown decided to sponsor an Easter pageant. The idea was to take the amazing story of Easter and put it into a play that would call people to Christ. Passion plays are nothing new, but this church's elders wanted the gospel to be clear in the performance. At the end, people would be given an opportunity to respond to the good news.

This goal required clever scripting to overcome the limitations of the stage. And, of course, the performance had to be entertaining. So there were songs and really good acting. Church members were called upon to build elaborate sets, and they worked tirelessly to meet a rigorous production schedule. Zoos and farms were emptied of animals and trainers. Camels, sheep, and cows walked the aisle to get to the stage, to the delight of the audience. Doves flew on cue, for the most part.

The pageant was presented annually, and as the years passed, its popularity soared beyond all expectations. As it became more popular, professional Hollywood producers were hired. Even the role of "Jesus" was played by a (non-Christian) Hollywood performer. Although the church had one of the biggest sanctuaries in the area, demand for seats outstripped supply. Free tickets were distributed for crowd control; there were weeks of performances, and command performances were added. People streamed in from outlying towns and from distant lands. The program took on a life of its own.

When it all came together, what a performance! No one slept through *this* telling of the gospel! The acting was superb, the singing professional. The animals enthralled the kids. The highlight, at least for my children, was when the white stallion reared up on stage as the centurion on horseback flashed his sword. (I never quite figured out how they got that scene from the Gospels.) After the crucifixion, done a bit more tastefully and "theatrically" than the real thing, "Jesus" was raised up to the rafters by means of a series of clever wires. It was all truly amazing!

There was just one problem: when the church looked at what had happened over the years, despite the program's popularity, it found that virtually no one had come to Jesus.

For all the massive expenditures of money, all the time spent building sets, hiring people, and meeting strict city codes for hoisting people on wires, all the thousands and thousands of people who attended, and all the sweeping up of animal poop, people were not coming to Jesus—at least not in any more numbers than one would expect during the regular preaching of the Word. So the church elders, wisely, shut the pageant down.

I bet it was a hard call. People love programs—just look at the attendance at this pageant. But the church decided, in the end, that if members spent half the time they had spent on the production in friendly evangelistic conversations with neighbors, coworkers, or fellow students, they would see a better response to the gospel and reach even more people. If you think about it, there is no way you could ever fit into your church sanctuary all the non-Christians with whom the members of your church are in contact weekly—no matter how big the sanctuary.

The fact is, most people come to faith through the influence of family members, small-group Bible studies, or a conversation with a friend after a church service: Christians intentionally talking about the gospel.

But when you take a cold, hard look at programs, things

just don't add up. For one, there is an inverse economic bang for the buck: the more money spent on the programs, the less fruit from evangelism. So, for example, when people under twenty-one (when most people come to faith) were asked how they came to be born again, only 1 percent said it was through TV or other media, while a whopping 43 percent said they came to faith through a friend or family member.[1] Just think of the cost comparison between a cup of coffee and TV programming. Or think of the effect: moms lead more people to Jesus than do programs.

Oddly, it seems evangelistic programs do *other* things better than evangelism: they produce community among Christians who take part in them, they encourage believers to take a stand for Christ, and they can enable churches to break into new places of ministry.

Yet we seem to have an insatiable hunger for programs to accomplish evangelism. Why? Programs are like sugar. It's tasty, even addictive. However, it takes away a desire for more healthy food. Though it provides a quick burst of energy, over time it makes you flabby, and a steady diet will kill you.

A strict diet of evangelistic programs produces malnourished evangelism. Just as eating sugar can make us feel as if we've eaten when we haven't, programs can often make us feel as if we've done evangelism when we haven't. So we should have a healthy unease with programs. We should use them strategically but in moderation, remembering that God did not send an event, he sent his Son.

What should we do? We want to have evangelism in community. We long to have friends alongside us when we share our faith. But at the same time, we see the limits, even the dangers, of programs. Is there some alternative?

I would like to make a case for something completely different, something that is both communal and personal: a culture of evangelism.

WHAT IS A CULTURE OF EVANGELISM?

I have lived cross-culturally for a good portion of my life, and if there's one thing I've learned, it's that it is next to impossible to understand a culture, any culture, by simply reading a book. So it is with definitions and instructions on a "culture of evangelism." Any explanation of it comes up short without real-world experiences to give it meaning.

Culture certainly has to do with shared ideas, a shared language, and a shared understanding of how to act. There are many expressions of culture: as broad as Chinese culture and as small as family culture. Culture is often invisible, especially to those who are in it. Similarly, a "culture of evangelism" in churches or fellowships has common biblical ideas, a biblical language, and shared biblical actions. This culture, too, is often invisible to those in it.

But when I talk with church leaders from around the world and tell them that I long for a "culture of evangelism," I don't need to define it. They understand me intuitively. They yearn for it, too. They long for their churches to be loving communities committed to sharing the gospel as part of an ongoing way of life, not by the occasional evangelistic raid event.

Though it's next to impossible to instruct someone about every action needed in a healthy culture of evangelism, I do think we can describe the yearnings we feel for it. So let's spend the rest of the chapter looking at those yearnings. Here are my top ten yearnings for a culture of evangelism:

1. A Culture Motivated by Love for Jesus and His Gospel

> For the love of Christ controls us, because we have concluded this: that one has died for all, therefore all have died; and he died for all, that those who live might no longer live for themselves but for him who for their sake died and was raised. (2 Cor. 5:14–15)

Evangelism often feels like pushing a ball uphill. But when I'm with people whose motivation for evangelism springs from a love for Jesus, the perception of evangelism changes. To be compelled by love to share the gospel individually is a beautiful thing, but when it happens in community, it's joyfully glorious. The need to badger people to share their faith evaporates. It becomes something we long to do. It becomes a way of thinking.

Recently I was with some friends who were encouraged about some new believers and how they were growing spiritually. Brian turned to Shanyl and said: "Shanyl, I've got to hand it to you. Danny was so hard-hearted to the gospel that most people would have given up, but you pursued him with amazing love, both for Danny and for Jesus. You didn't stop, and God used you. It's astounding now to see how the gospel has changed Danny's life."

As I listened to Brian encourage Shanyl, I was encouraged to remember the love I have for Jesus and his gospel, and I was reminded how much I want to share the gospel faithfully with others. The world, the flesh, and the Devil always oppose us in evangelism. But in a culture of evangelism, rooted in hearts of love for Jesus and his gospel, it feels as if the mountain tilts down a bit and we begin chasing the ball.

2. A Culture That Is Confident in the Gospel

> I am not ashamed of the gospel, for it is the power of God for salvation. (Rom. 1:16)

"I wonder when they lost their confidence in the gospel," my British friend mused.

This was not language I was used to using. "What do you mean?" I asked.

We were speaking about a parachurch ministry that once had been a vibrant center of gospel witness, but had lately fallen into lukewarmness—sadly, history is full of such stories.

He pulled at his chin with his thumb and forefinger, then said, "I mean, at what point did they start trusting gimmicks and worldly methods rather than the plain message of the gospel?"

I yearn for a culture of evangelism that never trades confidence in the gospel for confidence in techniques, personalities, or entertainment gimmicks. Those who oppose the gospel always tell Christians that the modern world has made it irrelevant. They chip away at Christians' confidence in the power of the gospel. They did that ages ago, in a world that doesn't look that modern anymore, and they do it today, and will until Jesus returns. The world tempts weak Christians to be ashamed of the gospel. I yearn for a culture of evangelism in which we build one another up and remind one another to put aside worldly practices and techniques of evangelism, placing our full confidence in the power of the plain message of the gospel.

3. A Culture That Understands the Danger of Entertainment

> Your people who talk together about you by the walls and at the doors of the houses, say to one another, each to his brother, "Come, and hear what the word is that comes from the LORD." And they come to you as people come, and they sit before you as my people, and they hear what you say but they will not do it; for with lustful talk in their mouths they act; their heart is set on their gain. And behold, you are to them like one who sings lustful songs with a beautiful voice and plays well on an instrument, for they hear what you say, but they will not do it. (Ezek. 33:30–32)

People talked about the ancient Israelite prophet Ezekiel in the social network of his day (by the walls and doors) and called to one another, "Hey, let's go hear the hot new show in town: Ezekiel's preaching!" They went to hear him as if he were a "lusty singer" or a great musical performer. They saw Ezekiel not as a prophet speaking to them about their salvation but as an entertainer. For all their enthusiasm about the performance, what was on their minds was sex and money, not obedience to God.

Doesn't that sound like a modern problem? To get people to show up for a church service today, we need only to post a titillating topic on Twitter, put together a rousing musical performance, or find a charismatic speaker who pulls at people's heartstrings—extra points if he's funny. It's not hard. But beware, God warned Ezekiel, and he warns us today: you may get a crowd through such methods, but you won't get their hearts. To get hearts is a work of the Spirit alone.

In a culture of evangelism, we don't mistake entertainment for ministry, or ministry for entertainment. We declare together the wonderful truths of God. We tell one another of his great salvation, his glory among the nations, and his marvelous works (Ps. 96:2–3). I long for a church that understands the dangers of entertainment and sees it for what it is: a lion crouching at the evangelical door, ready to devour us. We need a culture of evangelism that never sacrifices to the idolatry of entertainment, but serves up the rich fare found in the gospel of Christ.

4. A Culture That Sees People Clearly

From now on, therefore, we regard no one according to the flesh. (2 Cor. 5:16a)

How easy it is to adopt the culture of the world and regard people based on sexist, racist, or other superficial views. We tend to forget that those around us are flesh-and-blood people with real hurts, dreams, struggles, and loves. But Paul speaks of how our vision of people changes when we know Christ. We don't see them through the eyes of the world, as we once did, but through the eyes of God.

When we first moved into our neighborhood in Lexington, Kentucky, we genuinely desired to reach out to people around us. But our first encounter about spiritual things with our neighbor Tom, who lived three doors down, was less than promising. One day he saw me working in the yard and dropped by to visit. He held a mixed drink in one hand and a cigarette in the other. We were chatting about this and that, mostly about how great his yard looked, when my six-year-old son bounded up. "Smoking is dangerous—you need to quit," he blurted out with a frown on his face and hands on his hips. "Pray to Jesus, and he'll help you stop."

I stood speechless with a smile frozen on my face. "Oh, great!" I thought. "Where did that come from? They probably already think we're moralizing religious fanatics who sit around our table and talk about the evil neighbors." In David's defense, his Aunt Linda, a new believer, had committed to stop smoking, and David had been praying for her. Nevertheless, I was mortified.

But Tom ground out his cigarette, dropped to eye level with my son, and smiled as he put his hand on his shoulder. "You know what, David?" he said. "You're probably right, you're probably right."

What a gracious and wonderful response from Tom! It got me thinking about my view of him. I realized I needed to repent of thinking of Tom as just some guy down the street and see him for who he was. David's intro might have been rude, but it was better than my inaction, and it actually led to a relationship with Tom that I don't know would have happened if I hadn't started to see Tom as a real person.

When Paul says that we should see people through the eyes of Christ, he means for us to have a gospel view of people. So we see people as beautiful, valuable creatures made in the image of God. Each and every one of us carries God's mark. That is why Christians believe all people have dignity, worth, and value.

At the same time, we recognize that every person is fallen, sinful, and separated from God. All people have twisted the image of God into horrible shapes. That is why Christians are not enamored with people either.

But in a culture of evangelism, most of all we're mindful of what people can become: new creations in Christ, renewed and restored by the transforming power of God (2 Cor. 5:17). I long to be with Christians who remember that people are image-bearers. I long to be with Christians who remember people's separation from God. Most of all, I long for a culture that remembers what people can become through the gospel.

5. A Culture That Pulls Together as One

> I thank my God in all my remembrance of you, always in every prayer of mine for you all making my prayer with joy, because of your partnership in the gospel from the first day until now. (Phil. 1:3–5)

Paul wrote to the church of Philippi, telling them of his gratefulness to them for partnering with him in the ministry of the gospel. This is a picture of a culture of evangelism. They all pulled together for the gospel. Everyone was on game.

When I coached my five-year-old son's soccer team, we would gather the team (very, very cute) and ask, "Okay, team, when the other team has the ball, which of our players are on defense?" They would shout, with gusto, "Everyone!" Then we would ask, "And when we have the ball, which of our players are on offense?" "Everyone!" they answered. However, when it came to an actual game, putting that concept into play proved to be a bit more difficult with five-year-olds.

Evangelism is like that. But the goal for both is the same: for all to pull in the same direction together.

In a culture of evangelism, there is an understanding that everyone is engaged. Have you ever heard someone say, "Evangelism is not my gift," as if that excused him from sharing his faith? That's a kindergarten understanding of evangelism. All Christians are called to share their faith as a point of faithfulness, not gifting (Matt. 28:19).

I long to share my faith in the context of a church that understands what I'm doing and is pulling with me. In such a culture, when I bring a friend to church, others don't assume that person is a Christian. They are not shocked when I introduce someone and say, "This is Bob, and he's checking out Christianity." And not only are they not shocked, but they respond with something like this: "I'm so glad you are here. I was in the same place a couple of years ago, and I'd love to hear about it. Tell me, what are you thinking through?"

I long for a culture where we are all working together toward the goal of being witnesses for Christ.

6. A Culture in Which People Teach One Another

. . . always being prepared to make a defense to anyone who asks you for a reason for the hope that is in you. (1 Pet. 3:15b)

Follow the pattern of the sound words that you have heard from me, in the faith and love that are in Christ Jesus. (2 Tim. 1:13)

Peter instructs us to be ready to share reasons and answers for the hope within us. To be able to do this, we need thoughtful training, which we then put to use. This is why Paul reminds Timothy to follow what he's been taught.

I would happily trade all the pizzazz of stunning speakers, mind-blowing music, and wildly popular Easter pageants for a culture of evangelism in which people are trained to lead a Bible study with a non-Christian in the Gospel of Mark, point to the message of the gospel in the text, and urge the unbeliever to come to Jesus based on the truth of what he has learned from the Scriptures.

In a culture of evangelism, members teach one another the kind of things we looked at in the previous chapter: what is evangelism, what is the gospel, and what is true biblical conversion. We also teach one another how to share the gospel message. Then we do it all over again, knowing that we get rusty. In a culture of evangelism, people carefully teach one another how to share their faith in a biblical way.

7. A Culture That Models Evangelism

What you have heard from me in the presence of many witnesses entrust to faithful men who will be able to teach others also. (2 Tim. 2:2)

The beautiful thing in a culture of evangelism, if we get it right, is that new believers have the zeal and the contacts that older Christians often lack. However, older Christians have the insight and knowledge that younger Christians need.

As I type, my wife is sitting on the couch preparing to meet with Ruth and Samanti this afternoon. Leeann is leading them both through *Christianity Explained*. Ruth is a new believer; she's excited about her faith and sharing the gospel. Ruth and Samanti work together and have a lot in common since they come from the same city in Sri Lanka. Samanti's father is Buddhist, her mother is Roman Catholic, and her husband is Muslim. This is typical of Dubai. As Ruth shared with Samanti about her Christian faith, Samanti told Ruth that she wanted to know more. Ruth is deeply aware that her life has been ransomed by Jesus, but when it comes to explaining her faith, she needs some help, especially with a person with Samanti's background. So she wisely brought Samanti to Leeann.

Leeann, on the other hand, is an evangelist with a wealth of knowledge and understanding, but her circle of friends, for the most part, is made up of mature Christians. Leeann was thrilled to meet and talk to Samanti. And Samanti needs Jesus!

The three of them are a great example of what happens in a culture of evangelism. Leeann takes the lead in explaining the gospel. Ruth learns about sharing her faith as she participates in the study and continues to nurture her friendship with Samanti. And, Lord willing, Samanti hears and responds to the amazing message that Christ saves sinners. In a culture of evangelism, people model evangelism for one another.

8. A Culture in Which People Who Are Sharing Their Faith Are Celebrated

> I hope in the Lord Jesus to send Timothy to you soon, so that I too may be cheered by news of you. For I have no one like him, who will be genuinely concerned for your welfare. For they all seek their own interests, not those of Jesus Christ. But you know Timothy's proven worth, how as a son with a father he has served with me in the gospel. (Phil. 2:19–22)

I love how Paul honors Timothy for his work in the gospel. In a similar way, John, who pastors another church in our city, regularly starts a fellowship time by asking for stories from those who had opportunities to speak about Jesus that week. After they share, he has someone pray for them.

This practice of celebrating evangelistic efforts is simple and doesn't take much time, but it's hugely important in developing a culture of evangelism. There is nothing so discouraging as feeling that a church is more interested in manning the nursery than sharing the faith.

I yearn to be in a church where even evangelistic attempts are championed. Even if an evangelistic effort doesn't lead to a gospel conversation, evangelistic failure is better than not trying evangelism at all.

9. A Culture That Knows How to Affirm and Celebrate New Life

> We always thank God, the Father of our Lord Jesus Christ, when we pray for you, since we heard of your faith in Christ . . . just as you learned it from Epaphras our beloved fellow servant. (Col. 1:3–4, 7)

Paul knew how to affirm new believers. He celebrated their conversion, but he kept his focus—and theirs—on Christ. He didn't elevate them inappropriately, but he didn't ignore them either. A culture of evangelism celebrates new life in Christ in the right way.

After a series of one-on-one meetings and Bible studies with Mark Dever, Rob rejected his former atheistic faith and told Mark that he had become a Christian. "Well, Rob," said Mark, "tell me what you mean." Rob explained the gospel and related how he had repented of his unbelieving way of life and put his complete trust in Christ.

Then Mark said: "Brother, from what you told me, I agree with you: you *have* become a Christian. Let's pray." After they prayed, Mark said: "You understand that the mark of true conversion is not a prayer, but a long-term walk with Jesus. So, even though I believe you have come to Christ, we'll see what happens as time goes on."

Mark's reply is an example of what I call the "'Hallelujah!' and 'We'll see'" response. We say "Hallelujah!" because true conversion is the best thing that can happen to a person. We say "We'll see" because we know that conversion can be counterfeit, even if unintentionally. The most important check is threefold: a good understanding of the gospel, a changed life, and a long-term walk with Christ.

Mark didn't keep Rob's conversion a secret, but neither did he elevate Rob as an instant celebrity. At his baptism, Rob shared, appropriately, how he had come to faith. But there were trials to come, and how he walked through them was more important than any conversion story.

In a culture of evangelism, Christians know how to respond to those who have recently come to faith.

10. A Culture Doing Ministry That Feels Risky and Is Dangerous

I want you to know, brothers, that what has happened to me has really served to advance the gospel, so that it has become known

> throughout the whole imperial guard and to all the rest that my imprisonment is for Christ. (Phil. 1:12–13)

Paul's ministry was risky enough that he was thrown in jail. Likewise, I live in a part of the world where I actually know people who have gone to jail because they have lived faithful lives in Christ.

As we see in 2 Corinthians 10:5, Paul saw the Christian life as waging war on thoughts opposed to God: "We destroy arguments and every lofty opinion raised against the knowledge of God, and take every thought captive to obey Christ." This is risky; the world doesn't like to have its thoughts challenged. Are we willing to call people to risky evangelism? I long for a culture of evangelism that is risky in the sense that we're confronting culture. Mostly that means disregarding what people think of us.

Door of Hope Church in Portland, Oregon, is reaching out to hipsters with great effect. The church leadership even decided to take its Sunday evening service to a nearby park. It was the regular service, just held in the open air. They faced sneers, hecklers, and a woman who stripped off her top to try to shock the congregation. But others, who saw the kindness and love in the church, joined them.

Others take different kinds of risks. My friend Joanna says, "I don't even know how to do Bible study without a couple of Muslims in the group." We should all think through ways we can take risks in our particular contexts. A funny thing happens when we take risks: we become dangerous—that is, in the spiritual realms—to those who have their minds set against God.

In Philippians, Paul says the gospel had become known among the imperial guard (Phil. 1:13). And when he sends greeting at the end of the book, he writes, "All the saints greet you, especially those of Caesar's household" (4:22). It's clear that Paul had seen some of his guards come to faith.

Paul risked, and his risky life for the gospel was a path to jail. But I've always loved the observation that it was not so much that Paul was chained to a guard, but that a guard was chained to Paul.

I long for a church where neighboring atheists and non-Christians see fellow atheists and non-Christians coming to faith—an indication that we're a part of a risk-taking culture of evangelism.

11. A Culture That Understands That the Church Is the Chosen and Best Method of Evangelism

> And day by day, attending the temple together and breaking bread in their homes, they received their food with glad and generous hearts, praising God and having favor with all the people. And the Lord added to their number day by day those who were being saved. (Acts 2:46–47)

Okay, I know I said ten things. But there is one more, one that has run through all the other ten: I long for a church that understands that it—the local church—is the chosen and best method of evangelism. I long for a church where the Christians are so in love with Jesus that when they go about the regular time of worship, they become an image of the gospel. I long for a church that disarms with love, not entertainment, and lives out countercultural confidence in the power of the gospel. I long for a church where the greatest celebrations happen over those who share their faith, and the heroes are those who risk their reputations to evangelize.

I yearn for a culture of evangelism with brothers and sisters whose backs are up to mine in the battle; where I'm taught and I teach about what it means to share our faith; and where I see leaders in the church leading people to Jesus. I want a church where you can point to changed lives, where you can see people stand up and say, "When I came to this church two years ago, I didn't know God, but now I do!" I long to be a part of a culture of evangelism like that. I bet you do, too.

I mentioned earlier that I do not think programs are the best or even the primary way we should do evangelism. What I do think is that the best outreach happens in a culture of evangelism inside a healthy church. This is far too big a topic for just one of the top ten; the role of the church and the way of evangelism is our next chapter.

3

CONNECTING CHURCH
AND A CULTURE
OF EVANGELISM

As I mentioned earlier, if you are a part of a healthy church that has a culture of evangelism, you are a part of the greatest way of evangelism ever known. How is this principle worked out in the church?

Put aside pragmatic objections to this idea; we are dealing with a deeply spiritual, biblical concept. Jesus said, "By this all people will know that you are my disciples, if you have love for one another" (John 13:35). A little later, during the same time with his disciples, he prayed that they would be unified, "so that the world may believe that you have sent me" (John 17:20–21). Jesus says the love we have for one another in the church is a statement that we are truly converted. And when we are unified in the church, we show to the world that Jesus is the Son of God. Love confirms our discipleship. Unity confirms Christ's deity. What a powerful witness!

There are many Scripture passages that instruct and shape our evangelistic efforts, but these verses are foundational because they show us that the church is to be a culture of evangelism. We should use them to catechize our children!

Q: What action affirms our genuine conversion in Christ?
A: Loving other Christians.

Q: And how do we show that Jesus is the Son of God?
A: Uniting with other believers.

THE LOCAL CHURCH IS THE GOSPEL MADE VISIBLE

If we are to picture the gospel in our love for one another, that needs to take place in a local congregation of people who have covenanted together in love to be a church. It's not abstract love, but love for people in the real world. I can't tell you how many times I have heard from non-Christian people that the church was strange to them, but what drew them into the fellowship was the love among the members.

But the gospel is pictured not just in our love. Have you ever thought of how many biblical instructions God has built into the fabric of the church that, if done correctly, serve as proclamations of the gospel?

In pursuing a healthy culture of evangelism, we don't remake the church for evangelism. Instead, we allow the things that God has already built into the church to proclaim the gospel. Jesus did not forget the gospel when he built the church.

For instance, baptism pictures the death, burial, and resurrection of Jesus. It shows how his death is our death and his life our life. The Lord's Supper proclaims the death of Christ until he returns and prompts us to confess our sins and experience forgiveness anew. When we pray, we pray the truths of

God. We sing the great things God has done for us through the gospel. We give financially to advance the gospel message. The preaching of the Word brings the gospel.

In fact, the preaching of the Word of God is what forms the church to begin with. And, once formed, the church is given the task of making disciples, who then are sent to preach the gospel to form new churches. This cycle has been happening since Jesus ascended into heaven and will continue until he returns.

A REAL HIGH POINTE

Recently, I was at High Pointe Baptist Church in Austin, Texas. The pastor, Juan, had asked me to do a seminar on developing a culture of evangelism. I talked and people asked questions. Then someone asked an elephant-in-the-room type of question: "Many Vietnamese are moving into the community around our church; what is the church going to do to reach out to them?"

On the one hand, this was a wonderful question. A member had recognized that she had the privilege and responsibility to reach out with the gospel, and she saw an opportunity to do it. On the other hand, the way the question was phrased seemed to imply that reaching out was the responsibility of the church, not the person who had noticed the opportunity.

But a culture of evangelism is grassroots, not top-down. In a culture of evangelism, people understand that the main task of the church is to be the church. We've already seen that church practices are a witness in and of themselves. Certainly the church supports and prays for outreach and evangelistic opportunities, but the church's role is not to run programs. The church should cultivate a culture of evangelism. The *members* are sent out from the church to do evangelism. I know this may seem a bit picky, but it's really important. If you don't get this right, you can subvert the church—or be wrongly angry with church leadership.

Here's how I responded to the question at High Pointe: "It's really not the best thing for 'the church' to set up programs for Vietnamese outreach, but rather for you to think how you can reach out. I would recommend you learn something about the Vietnamese culture, maybe by learning some greetings in Vietnamese, trying their food, and learning about the struggles they face living in the majority culture. Reach out and invite the friends you make to come with you to your homes, a small-group Bible study, or church. Then, perhaps, some of you should even think of moving into the Vietnamese community with the purpose of commending the gospel among that community."

I was met with blank stares. But there was great relief on the face of Pastor Juan, who was grateful that I had not just singlehandedly set up an outreach program for him to run.

Then I added: "And when you bring your friend from the community into church, everyone is 'on game': you are all reaching out. That's a culture of evangelism. It's not just about being friendly, though that needs to happen, but having a deep awareness that we are in this together. In a healthy church, visitors see the gospel present in all we do. That's why we sing the Word, pray the Word, preach the Word. We want people to hear the gospel in the service. And when we practice the sacraments, we want them to see the gospel and hear it again as we explain what's happening. As members live out the gospel, the gospel comes out of us."

That's a sketch of a culture of evangelism at work. I know it's a bit radical—and I didn't even suggest they enroll their kids in the local school with the Vietnamese kids. Some might accuse me of not caring for the Vietnamese community because I told High Pointe not to set up a church-sponsored outreach. But I would argue that the best way to care for that community or any community is to give them the gospel so they can come to faith. That goal is best served by the witness of a church that has a culture of evangelism, by members making friends with Vietnamese people with whom they can then share the gospel. This approach has a far greater impact than a church program for clothing distribution, day care, going door to door, bringing in a kiddy carnival, or any other of the various good-hearted things churches do.

In one sense, all churches have a culture of evangelism of one kind or another. Even churches that reject evangelism have a culture of evangelism, though an unbiblical one. The question is not, "Do we have a culture of evangelism?" but "Is our culture of evangelism sick or healthy?"

I would like to make the case that the biggest reason churches' evangelism cultures are sick is not that we have a fear of man or that we don't have the right strategy or method of evangelism—as big as those issues may be—but that we do not understand the church.

ONE OR TWO DEGREES OFF TAKES YOU WIDE OF THE MARK

One of my great joys when I was directing a short-term trip for students in Kenya was flying with a missionary pilot who helped us with the program. Pete had been flying since the

EVANGELISM

days before GPS, when a pilot navigated by a compass and the seat of his pants.

Pete would fly our students into the most remote places for their assignments. Sometimes there was a space in the plane for me to tag along. After we dropped the student off, I would become Pete's co-pilot. Pete would take off, level the plane, and give me the compass setting. I would fly the plane through the Great Rift Valley, over the Masai Mara reserve, and around Mount Kenya, which towered high above as we flew past. Pete enjoyed pointing out sights and I reveled in the scenery. What joy!

Flying is actually not that difficult. It's landing that's hard, so Pete did that part. My job was just to keep the plane at altitude and steer toward the compass heading. I flew in the right general direction, but I hardly excelled. Occasionally Pete would check the compass heading and seem annoyed. He would thump on the glass pane of the compass and state brusquely, "You're off heading." I thought he was being picky until Pete said, "Mack, you need to understand, two degrees off takes us to another country."

It's true. Looking at a map or globe easily confirms the big problems that can result from small course deviations. And the same is true in the church.

The root problem with the question at High Pointe was not that the woman didn't understand evangelism; the problem was that she didn't understand the church. She was only a couple of degrees off, but that couple of degrees had taken her to another place. Understanding the church helps us get the right compass heading for evangelism. So we first need to think about the church and what makes it healthy.

DEFINING CHURCH

Say you were shopping at the mall and someone with a clip-board and pen asked, "Please define 'church' to the best of your ability." Could you answer? If he asked a follow-up question, "What are the necessary and sufficient components of a church?" would you be stumped?

If so, you're not alone. I have been living with and visiting missionaries around the world for decades. Many of these people call themselves church planters. They are amazing, wonderful people, yet I'm often just as amazed at how few of them are able to define a church biblically. When they do explain church, their definitions are based on their own feelings and human strategies.

I love Acts 29 churches;[1] I wish there were more of them. But unfortunately, what we have in so many places around the globe is not "Acts 29" churches but what I call "Judges 22" churches: churches that do what is right in their own eyes (Judg. 21:25). In their place, we need churches firmly rooted in the Scriptures.

I was with a missionary who was leading a church-planting team in Russia. He was, and is, a wonderful brother in Christ. He is deeply committed to the work of the gospel. He is servant-hearted and sacrificial. Further, he's a leader who is deeply influencing the people with whom he works. When he told me that his primary calling was to plant churches, I was thrilled. But as I asked questions about the church, he didn't seem to know what direction to go. Finally, in frustration, he said, "Well, okay, how would you define a church?"

"Well," I said, "the critical components of a church are best understood within three categories: what the church is, what the church does, and what is the mission of the church." It turned out to be a late night as we talked through church. In brief, here's what I told him.

The Christian faith has no category for believers who are not members of a local congregation. Church is not, and has never been, optional for the believer.[2] But even given that the church plays such a fundamental role in our discipleship, the average church member has an astounding variety of ideas about what church should be—ideas not rooted in the Bible.

Certainly churches have the freedom to do many things. Churches are free to build buildings or meet in rented ballrooms, to let the congregation sit in pews or on the floor. They're also free, under the authority of the Word, to devise specific strategies for fulfilling broad biblical commands. So they're free to provide music ministries, sponsor soup kitchens, host men's prayer meetings, run Christian schools, or develop small groups.

But what are the critical components, the things that are both necessary and sufficient? If you strip out everything, what are the irreducible parts of a church? This is easy to figure on many points. For instance, take away the Christian school and you still have the church. But take away the regular preaching of God's Word—no church.

Every Christian should know what makes a church a church. And a scriptural answer to what makes a church a church is surprisingly simple, at least on paper.

What the Church Is

A local church is a gathering of baptized, born-again Christians who covenant together in love to meet regularly under the authority of the Scriptures and the leadership of the elders to worship God, be a visible image of the gospel, and, ultimately, to give God glory (John 3:1–8; 13:34–35; Acts 2:41; 14:23; Eph. 3:10; Col. 3:16; 2 Tim. 3:16–17; Heb. 10:24–25).

What the Church Does

A church must do only a few things to be a church: the people regularly gather in gospel love to hear the Word preached, sing, pray, give, and practice the sacraments of baptism and the Lord's Supper. Members, those who have covenanted together, lovingly care for one another (1 Cor. 12:12–26), even through the practice of church discipline (Matt. 18:15–17).

The Mission of the Church

The church is God's strategic plan for evangelism with one overarching mission: to go to all peoples to make disciples, teaching them to obey everything Christ has commanded—including forming new churches (Matt. 28:18–20).

There it is: four sentences about the church that took me less than a page to write but take us all a lifetime to live. But this definition chops out what so many think the church is. It is not a building; neither is it a mere social gathering of believers. It requires a commitment to one another in a local community. A church does not intentionally have non-Christians as members. And only those baptized should be members.

A church is not a marketplace of good ideas for living well, but a fellowship submitted to the Word of God.

A HEALTHY CHURCH

So we have just defined a church. Now let's look at a healthy church.

It's important to say that the above marks do not describe a perfect church, which doesn't exist on this side of heaven. Neither are we trying to distinguish a true church as opposed to a false church. Rather, we want to distinguish between true churches that are sick and true churches that are healthy, and we want to help sick churches get well.[3]

There are all too many ways in which Christians can ignore basic foundations of a healthy church:

- Motivational speeches can be given rather than the preaching of God's Word. If preaching is about good thoughts for the day or living a moral—or worse, prosperous—life, and not about the Bible, people will not understand God and his ways.
- Conversion can become hazy, undefined, and subjective, which means people who are not Christians are taught that they are. And so non-Christians become members. When that happens, the church cannot practice biblical evangelism.
- Membership can be seen as optional. However I can't love people—beyond a romanticized theoretical love—if I don't know who they are. I must commit myself to them and they to me.
- Non-believers can be given positions of leadership in a church. Do I even need to say anything more about that? Yet it happens regularly, especially in churches that don't have membership.

- Hard stuff can go undone. Too often we fail to love people we don't like. Or we fail to practice church discipline with those we do.

Any one of these practices may not seem that big a deal, but if a church falls into any of these ways, soon it will be flying in the *opposite* direction of its compass heading. There is so much at stake in this because sometimes good-hearted people become blind guides and reproduce "Judges 22" churches. To make matters worse, when the foundations are discarded and a church becomes unhealthy, the glory of God is hidden. What is meant to be the beauty of Christ's community as a witness before the watching world is lost.

We need to touch on one other serious problem that leads to a sick church and has a direct impact on a culture of evangelism. It is when members confuse their personal obedience in evangelism and the role of the church.

PERSONAL PRIORITIES, CHURCH PRIORITIES, AND SHOE BOXES

In a healthy culture of evangelism, it's understood that there is a different priority for the church and for the individual. Something you should do in evangelism personally might not be the best thing for the church to do as a whole. This is the underlying reason for my answer to the question of outreach at High Pointe.

Here's an example of what I mean. Pastor Jacky is a friend of mine who works with a Chinese-speaking church in Dubai. He's done amazing work among the poor Chinese who come to the city as laborers. One year around Christmas, some good-hearted Westerners had the idea to distribute shoe boxes to the laborers. There is certainly nothing wrong with that. So families in Dubai churches put soap and washcloths, some cologne, combs, and a couple of other personal grooming items, along with some small items of clothing, into shoe boxes. They also put in flyers for the church's service and wrapped the boxes with Christmas bows. Again, no problem.

Then people were recruited to collect the boxes and—here's the kicker—deliver them to Jacky. I remember dropping by Jacky's office and not being able to get in the door because of all the shoe boxes—floor to ceiling shoe boxes.

Put aside questions about the biblical basis for the outreach or how effective it was; put aside questions concerning the long-term good, or even what statement was being made by rich Westerners giving grooming items to poor laborers. The root issue was that Jacky could not prepare his sermon. He could not meet with people who wanted to talk with him about Jesus. He could not fulfill his ministry and equip the church members for theirs because people did not understand that it was their role to reach out and Jacky's role to preach, shepherd, and pray. The people mistook their role *in* the church for the role *of* the church.

Let's say that the shoe box ministry did the best thing possible and people came to the Chinese church. When they did, what kind of church would you hope they encountered? A healthy church, where they heard the gospel in the preaching of the Word, where members were discipled and were "on game" in evangelism, where the gospel was presented in baptism, the Lord's Supper, and more? Or a sick church, where the leaders spent all their time delivering shoe boxes?

If Jacky were to spend all his time delivering shoe boxes and not attending to the work given to him to nurture a healthy church, he would be letting the church lie fallow. This is true not just of Jacky but of any elder of any church. Members are free to do many other things, but they must be very careful to support the leadership so that the church goes in the right direction.

The well-meaning believers in Dubai did not distinguish between the church's responsibility and their own. They believed the church should reach out to the laborers in the same way they wanted to reach out personally. But by acting on this assumption, they actually subverted the church.

A biblical example of this kind of issue is found in Acts 6, where we learn that the Greek widows were left out of the early church's daily distribution of food. One suspects the Hebrew widows were receiving the food because they had Jewish connections that the Greek widows did not have. Regardless, this situation needed attention. So the apostles asked *the concerned members* to select seven godly men to handle the case.

All these men were Greeks, as evidenced by their names, which was a sure-fire way to end any cronyism or racism. But note why the apostles took care of this injustice in the way they did. They said:

"It is not right that we should give up preaching the word of God to serve tables. Therefore, brothers, pick out from among you seven men of good repute, full of the Spirit and of wisdom, whom we will appoint to this duty. But we will devote ourselves to prayer and to the ministry of the word." (Acts 6:2–4)

So individual church members were called to step up and solve a problem themselves in order to protect the primary ministry of the church's leaders: the ministry of the Word and prayer.

Church members must understand the priorities the apostles guarded. Though there are many important things the church body can do—as important as feeding widows—nothing should subvert the primary calling of the church: to preach the Word. Members and pastors alike should come alongside one another and protect the unique and primary calling of the church.

HOW A HEALTHY CULTURE OF EVANGELISM CONNECTS WITH A HEALTHY CHURCH

How, then, does a healthy culture of evangelism work? Here's just one example:

Abigail, a full-time mom, sat on the bus going to Washington, D.C., from the Dulles airport. It had been a long trip back from a funeral in Texas, and she looked forward to being with her family. She was sitting next to a young Asian woman. But rather than burying herself in a book, she struck up a conversation.

The girl's name was Van. As they spoke, Van told Abigail that she had just arrived from China, and these were her first few hours in America. Abigail knew a divine appointment when she saw one. She wanted to reach out, but she knew she needed to be sensitive, too.

As she thought through things going on at her church, she remembered an upcoming wedding of two strong believers. She knew the gospel would be presented there. The church encourages all members to come and bring friends to hear the witness of a wedding. So Abigail asked, "Would you be interested in coming to a Christian wedding?" Sure enough, Van jumped at the chance. They exchanged emails and Abigail arranged to pick Van up.

Notice that Abigail trusted in a healthy culture of evangelism. There was no need to call up the pastor and pressure the staff to start a church program for Chinese evangelism. She didn't have to wonder whether the gospel would be clear at the wedding. In a church with a healthy culture of evangelism, the gospel saturates all ministries. Abigail picked a wedding, but she could have invited Van to any number of things.

Sure enough, the wedding focused as much on the Bridegroom of heaven as the bride and groom on earth. Both the couple and the pastor shared the gospel. But best of all, after the service was over and the reception began, Abigail took her four-year-old out to the church playground, and Van went with them. Van began asking questions about what made a Christian wedding different from a secular wedding. Abigail, well schooled in the gospel message, took the opportunity to explain from the wedding the entire gospel to Van.

Abigail then asked Van if she would like to have a Bible. Since the church stocked Bibles for international students at its bookstall, the two of them walked back into the church and Abigail gave Van a Bible in Mandarin, the first Bible Van had ever seen. Abigail then offered to get together with Van and read the Bible, which they did. Abigail even invited some church members who spoke Mandarin to meet with Van and share their testimonies during one of their Bible readings. When they did, Van was touched and asked penetrating questions.

Abigail and Van continued reading the Bible and talking about the gospel until Van left for school in Boston a few weeks later. But Abigail wasn't finished. She had a friend in Boston, who agreed to continue reading the Bible with Van. That's happening as I write these words.

Abigail didn't wait for the church to do something. She didn't even think about that. She put her confidence in the church being the church. She leaned on the power of the gospel and trusted the Holy Spirit to work through her faithful steps as an ambassador of Christ.

That's how a culture of evangelism functions in a church. It's not flashy, it's not a program, but it's so much better.

4

INTENTIONAL EVANGELISTS IN A CULTURE OF EVANGELISM

Kelly, a sixteen-year-old, traveled from her home country of Brazil to attend high school as an exchange student in Portland, Oregon. Connie and John, Kelly's American host parents, were pleasant, easygoing people who regularly attended a gospel-centered church. Kelly was a good student and, coming from a Japanese/Brazilian background, she was comfortable with multiple cultures, so she moved with ease in her Portland high school.

Connie and John prayed for Kelly and took her to church, but Kelly didn't seem interested in the Christian faith. Yet John and Connie became dear to Kelly, so after she returned home, they kept in touch. Connie prayed for her over the years—years that stretched from five to ten to fifteen.

Recently, Leeann and I were asked to speak at John and Connie's church, Hinson Baptist. At lunch after the service, Connie happened to sit next to Leeann. "Long ago," Connie told Leeann, "we hosted an exchange student named Kelly who is now a flight attendant with Emirates Airlines. She's a very sweet girl." (Never mind that Kelly was now a grown woman.) "She lives in Dubai. Do you think you can be in touch with her? She's going through a bit of a lonely time as she's just broken up with her boyfriend."

Leeann was delighted to get in touch with Kelly, but it was going to be a number of weeks before we returned home to Dubai. So Connie and Leeann both wrote Kelly and told her about our church, Redeemer. On Connie's recommendation, Kelly found Redeemer and went to church before Leeann even returned.

When Kelly walked in, she was immediately greeted by Hetty, from the Philippines, who manned the welcome table, and then Kanta, from India, at the book stall. Kelly listened to Pastor Dave preach the gospel and her heart was strangely warmed. Afterward, Hetty and Kanta (who did not know that Kelly was a contact from our travels in the United States) invited her to lunch. When Kelly went home, she opened her welcome bag and found two books: *The Cross Centered Life* by C. J. Mahaney and *Two Ways to Live*, a gospel explanation by Philip Jensen and Tony Payne. She devoured them both. Later, Hetty and Kanta invited her to a small-group Bible study, where she was warmly received.

When Leeann returned to Dubai, she and Kelly had lunch. Kelly shared with Leeann about her life and how much she loved the church. She said, "I want to be a member." Then she asked, "Are there membership dues I need to pay?" Leeann smiled and said: "No, there are no dues for our church, but there is something very important you must understand to become a member. It's this thing we call the gospel."

"Oh, then tell me this gospel," said Kelly.

Multiple continents, a couple of churches, various cities, many languages, numerous ethnicities, diverse personalities, years of prayer, spoken and written communication, two lunches—one gospel. When I baptized Kelly in the hotel swimming pool where our church holds its baptisms, I couldn't help but cry for joy over everything God had orchestrated for his one lost daughter, Kelly.

Kelly was the one with the least idea that God was orchestrating people and events to bring her to himself. But she sees it now. In fact, she's joined the church welcome team because she expressly desires to reach out to those who don't know God. Just recently, Kelly met two flight attendants from Brazil who came to church for the first time. Who knows how God has worked in their lives to bring them to that point? Who knows what God will do?

In a culture of evangelism, people who love Jesus work together as instruments in the grand symphony of God's work. We don't always know what the next piece will be—the Holy Spirit orchestrates that. But if we are focused on him and his direction, we get to be a part of his work in people's lives.

It's too easy to play to the audience and not to the conductor. Remember, the Lord is our conductor. Be intentional in evangelism: follow Christ's lead. There are many ways to be distracted and to move off key. But in a maturing culture of evangelism, people trust God to do something bigger than what they see with physical eyes.

DIFFERENT PARTS, SAME GOAL

In a culture of evangelism, we call believers to walk in faith and be open to God's work in people around them. As part of this calling, church members must take a long-term view. The people around Kelly trusted God to work through them as they walked with Christ. So let's look at the different people who figured in her story and see what we can learn from these examples.

Connie did not give up on friendship over time, but prayed and waited for an opportunity. It came, though it took fifteen years. Don't be lulled into thinking that people are what they seem to be. Don't believe it for a minute. We bring the words of life to those who are desperate and dying, no matter how they look on the outside. So be prayerful and watchful, personally and corporately.

Kanta and Hetty didn't think of themselves as evangelists, but they were. They were kind and thoughtful "stealth" evangelists who had their feet shod with gospel readiness (Eph. 6:15).

Pastor Dave faithfully preached the gospel, as he does week in and week out. The people in the congregation know that when they bring their friends and family members to church, they will hear the gospel. Dave often says from the pulpit: "Those of you who are here today from other faith backgrounds, we want you to know how glad we are that you have come. I'd encourage you to talk about the sermon with me or any of the elders, or the people who brought you to church."

The small-group Bible study that Kelly attended was a warm and personal place to look at the Scriptures.

Leeann did not blow off the opportunity that came her way. It would have been easy to think that a relationship that was fifteen years old would prove to be a dead end and not worth her time. But Leeann was equipped to share the gospel, and then to probe and ask questions.

No one asked Kelly to "cross the line." There were no high-pressure techniques. At one point, when Leeann was talking with Kelly, Leeann confirmed that Kelly understood and had committed herself to the gospel. But if you asked Kelly who led her to Christ, she might be confused by the question. She might say "the Holy Spirit" or "a bunch of people."

In a culture of evangelism, the goal is for everyone to share, pray, and take opportunities as they come. We can challenge people to come to faith, but there are no instructions in the New Testament for a sinner's prayer. We trust God to bring sinners to repentance. Our responsibility is to be faithful witnesses—together.

How can we be a part of a vibrant culture of evangelism like that? How can we become intentional evangelists living in intentional cultures of evangelism? What sorts of platforms do we need to put in place so that we are prepared to share the gospel? I think there are six:

1. Prepare our hearts, minds, and feet
2. Understand a gospel-shaped way of life
3. Slay our assumptions
4. See evangelism as a discipline
5. Pray
6. When possible, give leadership in evangelism

1. PREPARE FOR SHARING: HEARTS, MINDS, FEET

In my first book on evangelism, *Speaking of Jesus,* I noted that there are three areas in which we need to check ourselves in evangelism: Are we motivated? Are we equipped? Are we available? These three questions help to ensure that our hearts, minds, and feet, respectively, are ready to share the faith.

For instance, one might have flocks of non-Christian friends and be motivated to share, but feel shaky about the gospel message. On the other hand, one might be adept at the ins and outs of the gospel, but not know any non-Christians. Or one might know the gospel and many unbelievers, but be dull to the spiritual reality of the eternal judgment that those friends without Christ are facing.

Over the years, as I've been with people who have thought through the "motivated," "equipped," and "available" grid, I've found there are two main categories of people who feel stymied in sharing their faith. The first is those who avoid sharing their faith because of fear. There are multiple things they fear: not knowing what to say; being rejected or looking stupid; or making people feel awkward.

The second category is people who are isolated from non-Christians. There's a variety of reasons for this isolation: perhaps they have retreated into the warm Christian subculture; they find the lifestyles of unbelievers offensive; or they are, ironically, too busy with ministry.

Asking whether we are motivated, equipped, and available helps to diagnose our personal witness. But these are helpful criteria to diagnose our cultures of evangelism, too. Once we've done some diagnosis, we can look at some cures.

Motivated Hearts at Church

Just as we check our hearts for personal motivation, churches should consider their corporate motivation. Here are some questions you might find helpful:

- Is our church cultivating compassion for those who don't know Christ?
- Do our members need to be encouraged when non-Christian hearts seem so hardened?
- Are our members convinced that the gospel is what produces the greatest change the world can know in hearts, minds, and lives, and the community at large?

Sometimes we unwittingly motivate congregations with blunt instruments such as guilt. But we want church members to be motivated by what's taught in Scripture and to see their role as Christ's ambassadors, mediating between two warring factions with the offer of peace and reconciliation.

Equipped Minds at Church

Churches must also be sure to equip their members with the gospel. They must use their gatherings to regularly rehearse and think through the gospel—on all levels.

The gospel should be present in our songs. My daughter-in-law, Stephanie, told me that she sang a song at her graduation that's often sung in church services—"God of This City." Half of her classmates were Muslims, and they had no trouble singing the song with gusto. If people from other faith backgrounds can sing a song *with gusto* at a secular high school graduation, we can be pretty sure there's no gospel in the song.

"God of This City" is a fine song—certainly better than much of what plays in pop culture—but there's no gospel in it.

When I think back on the words of some of the songs I've sung at church through the years, I see there was no gospel in them either. That's why I'm grateful that our music leader at church is so careful to choose songs that focus on the message of the cross. He wants the gospel proclaimed through song.

The gospel should also be present in all our preaching. A pastor friend of mine came up to me after I preached in his church. He told the story of how an elder complimented one of his sermons just a few months before and talked about some of the ways he'd been challenged by the message. But then the elder said, "My only concern is that I didn't hear the gospel." Then my pastor friend said: "I want to do for you what he did for me. Mack, I loved your sermon. Technically it was superb. But you know, I'm not sure that someone could have come to faith through the words you said today." He was right, and I am so grateful for that brother's willingness to point out that flaw to me. Do our sermons help people see their sin and Christ's offer of redemption?

There are other areas of our corporate life to examine. Our public prayers should proclaim that the gospel is our source of hope in the midst of the concerns we're bringing before the Lord. We can approach his throne boldly because Jesus is our High Priest (Heb. 4:14–16). We can include teaching about the gospel in our Sunday classes, membership interviews, and discipleship groups. We can challenge church members to learn a basic gospel outline and show them how to share their testimonies. We can point out books and pamphlets that explain the gospel, publications that believers should read on their own or, better yet, with non-Christians.

These things are not hard to do, but they are easy to forget. To equip congregations, it's important that the gospel be thoughtfully present in all aspects of church life.

Available Feet at Church

Churches can consider whether they are corporately available to non-Christians simply by asking whether their fellowships are welcoming to non-Christians.

We need to be careful here. It's easy to go from being a welcoming church to becoming a church that jettisons the gospel in its desire to be "friendly." Unfortunately, many churches fall into this heresy when their main concern becomes the non-Christian rather than fidelity to the gospel. The quickest route to heresy and error is "relevant" evangelism. Good-hearted motivations that try to shape the church for the needs of man and not the glory of God are the death of biblical churches.

The church is called to be a cross-centered, gospel-focused, God-glorifying community to the praise of Christ. We cannot forget that the aim of the church is set on Jesus as the Christ, not seekers and their comfort. The old seeker-sensitive movement and its modern replacements have it backward: churches are called to concentrate on God, while individuals are called to be sensitive to seekers.

So are we individually encouraging one another to be on the lookout for unbelievers who attend our services? Are we prepared to welcome them and help them understand what a Christian worship service is about? Are we building friendships that are intentional with the gospel? It's so easy and dangerous to assume everyone at church is a Christian.

Availability is not only about moving our feet to be with non-Christians, but also checking the "attitude of the mind." Our tendency is to write off people in our minds: friends we think would never be interested in Christianity; colleagues who seem too sinful, "too far gone"; or family members who say conversations about "your religion" are off limits. When I start thinking this way, I need friends to remind me that no heart is too hard for the Holy Spirit.

So in a culture of evangelism, we think carefully about three things: how we motivate our hearts, how we equip our minds, and how we move our feet to action.

2. OUR GOSPEL WORLDVIEW: THE CENTRALITY OF THE GOSPEL

Churches must treat the gospel as a way of life. Gospel centrality is crucial to a culture of evangelism.

When the lowly freshman apostle, Paul, rebuked the senior, pillar-of-the-church apostle, Peter, it must have taken some gumption (Gal. 2:11–14). Peter, after all, had walked with Jesus for three years in Palestine. He had preached the message of grace in Acts 2 to open the doors of the first church. He had stared down the Sanhedrin, the very court that had put Christ to death mere weeks before.

But in Galatians, Paul tells us that fear of man caused Peter to stumble. He was slipping into law and forgetting that the grace of God had been extended to all. The issue, at first glance, was the dinner table, but Paul saw the deeper meaning. Peter's actions were at odds with justification by grace alone.

This account in Galatians is important in helping Christians understand the grace of God for us in Christ. Paul even says in Galatians 2:5 that this "family fight" between Peter and him preserved the gospel.

Paul uses a phrase that is extremely helpful for understanding how we keep our lives gospel-focused. Paul says Peter's "conduct was not in step with the truth of the gospel" (2:14). This small phrase opens an entirely new vista for us about the gospel. It tells us the gospel is not only a message of salvation but a way of life.

I've found that as we live out the gospel, sharing the gospel is much more a part of our lives. However, living out the gospel is not the same as moral living. They look similar on the surface; perhaps that's why even the apostle Peter could be confused. But trying to live a moral life is impossible. Living a gospel life is a gift from God.

How to Live Out the Gospel

Saying that we should live out the gospel and knowing how that works out are two different things. Fortunately, the Bible tells us how to do it. The New Testament often takes a gospel theme and applies it to our lives.

Some would argue that everything Paul does is an application of the gospel. It's a fair way to understand Paul's epistles: he preaches the gospel, then he talks about the implications of the gospel in our lives. An "implication" is not the gospel message itself, but something that flows from the gospel. For instance, Paul tells us that our forgiveness for one another is tied to the gospel: ". . . forgiving each other; as the Lord has forgiven you" (Col. 3:13). Our way of life is tied to the gospel: "let your manner of life be worthy of the gospel" (Phil. 1:27). Even how we work in positions of authority is directly linked with the gospel:

> You know that the rulers of the Gentiles lord it over them, and their great ones exercise authority over them. It shall not be so among you. But whoever would be great among you must be your servant, and whoever would be first among you must be your slave, even as the Son of Man came not to be served but to serve, and to give his life as a ransom for many. (Matt. 20:25–28)

So for Christians, how we forgive, how we live, how we work and lead, and, really, everything about our lives should be rooted in the gospel.

What does this have to do with a culture of evangelism? Well, everything.

Understanding the gospel as a way of life means making sure our lives align with the gospel in every part. This helps the gospel come out of us whether we are with believers or non-believers. If we live gospel-centered lives, we will find ourselves sharing the gospel. If our fellowships know how to apply the gospel in all of life, they will explode with gospel-centered evangelism.

3. KILL OUR ASSUMPTIONS

Assuming the gospel is deadly. I'm saying that as clearly and bluntly as I know how. When the gospel is assumed, we begin to think that everyone who shows up at church is a Christian.

However unlikely that may be, many people in churches be-have as if that's true.

That bad assumption leads to the next: there is no need to share, teach, or preach the gospel. Over time, confusion about the gospel grows: external actions are confused with genuine Christian faith. Morality becomes an expectation and not a re-sponse of love. The cross is treated merely as an example, not the place where God's wrath and love uniquely meet. Eventu-ally, the gospel is lost altogether.

This is a travesty in the Christian community. It is why Paul instructed Timothy to guard the gospel and to pass it on with care; he knew the gospel could be lost.

Don't let your assumptions kill your community witness—slay them now. If you are bored with the gospel, you need to take a deep look at the sin of your heart. More seriously, if the gospel does not resonate in your heart, check and see that you are truly converted.

Andrei came to our fellowship as a second-year university student. It was tempting to pull him into leadership because he had great experience in ministry. He had been a leader in his youth group, and the kids loved him. He was talented with the guitar. He was winsome, good-looking, and just an all-around good guy. As a son of a pastor, he knew all kinds of Christian lingo and Bible verses that served him well.

Well, they served him well until we started doing in-depth Bible study. We studied the book of Mark. Andrei was bored. He knew all the stories about Jesus, and each session seemed repetitive. But he began to have a restless, uncomfortable feeling—the Holy Spirit was working. While reading Mark 8, which recounts how Jesus healed a blind man with a second touch, Andrei was suddenly chilled with the realization that, though he had been around Jesus for many years, he could not "see" Jesus. Just as the blind man initially saw people "like trees, walking" (v. 24) and needed a second touch, so Andrei, who had spent so much time in Christian community, was not a true follower of Christ.

Andrei repented of sin, the most wicked and hard-hearted sin, the sin most difficult to root out, the sin most condemned by Jesus: spiritual pride and religious arrogance. Andrei's is one of the most miraculous conversions I have ever seen because his previous life had seemed so close to a true Christian life. Yet when Andrei put his complete faith and trust in Jesus, the change was evident. He was clear about the gospel. He was joyful where he previously had been only driven. Andrei is articulate now about what happened to him.

But think about what could have happened if the community had assumed the gospel. Andrei would have been put in leadership. Those around him would have continued to assume that he was a Christian. As a non-Christian, he would have been teaching children of the church and students in the fellowship. Worst of all, Andrei would have been lost in his sin even while the community affirmed his faith.

There will always be people in our churches who look like believers, which is why it's so important that we keep sharing the gospel. They tend to be the very ones who push back about how boring and repetitive it is to talk about the gospel.

There was a time when such complaints would have tempted me to jazz up our church gatherings. But now, when someone tells me that the gospel is boring or that we need to move on to more pertinent teaching, I take it as a yellow flag to push in and find out what he means. There are many pretenders to the faith. There are many more who have been falsely assured that they are Christians because of how they were raised, because they were involved in the church, or because they had high moral standards. Knowing this, I'm no longer tempted to be accommodating.

I'm going to be blunt again: stop assuming that everyone at your Christian gatherings is a Christian. Assume that non-Christians *are* there.

I recently spoke in chapel at the Southern Baptist Theological Seminary. It is a seminary with a strong evangelical commitment. I deeply admire the administration and faculty. I trust that its students are deeply committed to ministry. Nevertheless, I still wanted the gospel to be clear in my talk, if nothing more than as a model for those who would become pastors, but also for any guests who happened to be there. Frankly, I've lived too long and seen too many who were in ministry either fall away or come to faith to think that there were not some pretenders in the midst: seminarians who didn't really know Christ.

What about our children? Many children pray a sinner's prayer when they are five, but I have seen many of those same kids come to Christ when they get to university. And I've cried with many parents whose adult children are far from the faith even though they acted like Christians when they were growing up. Keep talking to your children about the gospel, both at home and at church.

Earlier we noted that the gospel must be clear in everything we do as church communities so that members will be equipped to share the gospel. But it also needs to be in everything we do so that non-believers may be brought to faith in Christ.

So we sing the gospel. We pay close attention to the words to make sure they declare truths about Jesus. I know a woman in our church who actually came to faith while singing a song about Christ's redeeming work.

We pray the gospel. Even when we pray before meals, we can acknowledge that, while we are grateful for sustenance, we are more grateful for the sustenance that comes to our souls through the gospel.

We preach the gospel. We've already mentioned that sermons need the gospel and that we need to check whether someone could come to faith by listening to the sermon. But are people encouraged to talk about the sermon after the service if they have questions? I was at a family gathering where the father said, "Okay, everyone, I want to hear one thing that was encouraging to you about the sermon today." We need more of that.

Look for the gospel in your Bible studies. It's there in the text. Trust Jesus when he says that all the Scriptures point to him (Luke 24:27). Don't ever assume everyone knows the good news of Jesus Christ. Too many people are going in and out of churches without hearing it. Let's not take that risk.

4. EVANGELISM AS A DISCIPLINE

Spiritual disciplines, such as prayer, Bible study, and gathering as a church community, are means of grace in our lives.

Christians who learn these practices early in their walk with Christ grow in their faith. God uses spiritual disciplines for our spiritual health. We grow when we practice them. Our Christian lives become sloppy when we don't.

But have you ever thought of evangelism as a spiritual discipline?

Don Whitney has written an excellent book about spiritual disciplines. He tells me that it is the only book that he is aware of that specifically says evangelism needs to be treated as a spiritual discipline. Here's what he says:

> Evangelism is a natural overflow of the Christian life. We should all be able to talk about what the Lord has done for us and what He means to us. But evangelism is also a *Discipline* in that we must discipline ourselves to get into the context of evangelism, that is, we must not just wait for witnessing opportunities to happen.
>
> Jesus said in Mt. 5:16, "Let your light shine before men, that they may see your good deeds and praise your Father in heaven." To "let" your light shine before others means more than simply "Don't do anything to keep your light from shining." Think of His exhortation as, "Let there be the light of good works shining in your life, let there be the evidence of God-honoring change radiating from you. Let it begin! Make room for it."[1]

Later Whitney says, "Unless we discipline ourselves for evangelism, it is very easy to excuse ourselves from ever sharing the gospel with anyone."[2] Whitney believes that the point of disciplining ourselves for evangelism is to plan for it—for Christians to actually put it into their schedule.

God uses such discipline. Maybe not the first time a witnessing opportunity presents itself, but as we discipline ourselves over time, there comes a day when we find ourselves in a thrilling discussion about Jesus with a non-Christian, about his saving power and what he can do for those who truly desire to know him and his forgiveness.

5. THE PLACE OF PRAYER

I love the quote attributed to Charles H. Spurgeon: "Lord, save the elect, and elect some more!" I love the prayer and the attitude. We don't know whom God is calling to himself. Praying for others to be saved keeps us mindful of that.

I prayed for my sister, Linda, for twenty years, and I almost gave up. But God, in his mercy, drew her to himself. This gives me hope that other family members and friends whom I've prayed for over many years might still come to faith.

I pray regularly, "Lord, don't let a year go by where I am not directly involved in seeing someone come to you in faith." God has been faithful to that prayer. If God should grant me more years on earth, when I get to heaven there may be fifty or sixty people that I was instrumental in seeing come to faith. What a joy that would be!

Make it a discipline to pray regularly for those who don't know Christ to come to him. Pray in church services, in small groups, in gatherings in homes, at special events, and as a part of your devotional time. I have a friend who says he tries to pray prayers like those the Puritans prayed, prayers "God would blush not to answer." Let the people around you know that the salvation of the lost is on your heart before God.

6. SPIRITUAL LEADERSHIP

One of the key elements for a culture of evangelism is the leadership of the church or fellowship. If it is important that the members be "on game," it is doubly important for the elders and pastors to lead by teaching and modeling evangelism.

Dave, my pastor, lives in a high-rise apartment building next to a shopping center. He calls the security guards and maintenance staff by name. He has met all the cashiers at the grocery store and all the servers at the Tex-Mex restaurant (his favorite). He gets his hair cut frequently so he can build a relationship with his barber.

Dave's a friendly guy, but simple friendliness is not his primary motivation in all these contacts. He's motivated by his concern for these people and a desire to talk to them about the gospel, which he does often. He regularly introduces me to people from his apartment complex who come with him to church and hear him preach. Then we both get to talk to them about the gospel. I always leave these conversations encouraged about sharing my faith.

Besides teaching and modeling, one of the most important things leaders can do is just talk about evangelism. If you are a pastor, it's important that you set aside a place in staff meetings and elder meetings to talk about your personal efforts to share our faith. Look for ways to pray and encourage evangelism in other church leadership gatherings.

I was leading a seminar on evangelism at a church. The pastor asked me what I thought was the most helpful part of the training for people. I said, "Just talking about evangelism is the most helpful."

He gave me a strange look.

"No," I said, "I mean it. It's really not that much about what I say, as important as that is. It's that you have taken time to think about evangelism. People carving out a half day, praying for non-Christian friends, and thinking about what they need to do to evangelize is much more helpful than any of my talking points. The fact that you, as a leader in this church, just set up this seminar in some ways makes the most important statement."

Pastor Pete regularly has people share about any evangelistic opportunities the people in his congregation have had over the previous week. When people realized it was going to happen weekly, they not only began coming to the meeting ready to share about the ways God had used them, they became more attuned to opportunities around them during the week. It's a simple way to keep evangelism on the front burner.

If evangelism is to be a front-burner issue in our churches, it needs constant encouragement, ongoing training, and long-term, focused leadership of the kind these pastors are providing in their congregations.

In this chapter, we've been looking at important preparations for sharing our faith. They are critical. But the goal is not to be prepared—it is to find ourselves in conversations with others where we are speaking the very words of life. Ideas for having such conversations are the subject of our next chapter.

5

ACTUALLY SHARING OUR FAITH

A few years into our marriage, I purchased a book about marriage. It was a book that I should have read before we got married and certainly had needed earlier in our marriage. Yet when I first picked it up, I read the table of contents and turned to the chapter that most interested me.

That chapter started out something like this: "This chapter is the chapter that many of you have turned to first, before reading the previous chapters, but I want to encourage you to start from the beginning." He nailed me.

How did the author know I would turn to that chapter first? It was the chapter on sex.

Admittedly, that chapter about sex was a bigger draw than this chapter about actually sharing our faith, but I suspect that there are many who will turn to this chapter before reading the previous chapters. If you are one of them, well, good for you! I'm not going to tell you to go back and read the other chapters.

I appreciate that you want to get to it. I'm trusting that you can define evangelism, the gospel, and biblical conversion.

You have rejected programmatic and pragmatic evangelism, and see the compelling call to a culture of evangelism. You see the church as God's great plan for evangelism and that developing a culture of evangelism in the context of the church is the best thing we can do for the proclamation of the gospel. I trust you've prepared yourself to be an intentional evangelist because you see the gospel as a way of life, you never assume the gospel, you treat evangelism as a spiritual discipline, and you are in prayer for your friends who don't know Jesus. Those of you in leadership lead in evangelism by teaching it and doing it.

Wonderful. Of course, if any of those points are new concepts for you or are a bit fuzzy in your mind, you might want to start at the beginning. Regardless, we come to this chapter—the chapter about actually speaking about Jesus.

TALKING LIKE AN AMBASSADOR

To me, there is no better instruction for how we speak about Jesus than Paul's illustration of ambassadorship in 2 Corinthians 5:20–21:

> Therefore, we are ambassadors for Christ, God making his appeal through us. We implore you on behalf of Christ, be reconciled to God. For our sake he made him to be sin who knew no sin, so that in him we might become the righteousness of God.

Paul calls us to remember the power behind the message: Christ himself. We are told of our astounding responsibility to be representatives of the kingdom of God. We are Christ's ambassadors. We are called to see people differently—to give up the human and worldly vision of others and to know and love them, understanding that they are lost sinners who need to be reconciled to God.

We must get the message right. After all, ambassadors don't have the freedom to change the message; their job is to deliver it accurately. Likewise, we must not add to or subtract from Christ's message. We must correctly deliver the message so that sinners can be reconciled with the holy God, the Creator of the universe, the one who owns us and all those around us. Despite the fact that our sin is evil before him, he made a way of salvation by making him who knew no sin *to be sin*—that is, taking on our sin—and to receive the just punishment of God on our behalf on the cross. This was so that in Jesus we might become the righteousness of God. We can be restored to a right relationship with God by simply believing Christ, repenting of sin, and turning to him in faith. This is the message we have been given to deliver.

We must deliver the message regardless of the discomfort produced, effort required, and shame endured. Ambassadors *exist* to deliver messages. So we shout out, "Be reconciled to God." We may not feel like representatives of the kingdom of God, but that is what we are. It is how we are seen in the spiritual realms, and it's an astounding truth.

Of course, we can be good or bad ambassadors. If you are reading this book, I'm assuming you want to do well in this role, so let's think through some ways that we can be better at what we are called to do.

AMBASSADORS AND THEIR APPROACH: THINKING THROUGH CONVERSATIONS

Here is a letter I received that touched my heart. As you read it, think about how you might have responded:

Dear Mack,

I've been praying for Candice for a while now—for opportunities to share the gospel. A little background: Candice was raised Catholic but does not go to any church currently. She lives a homosexual lifestyle in the context of a family with four kids. The kids are biologically her partner's, but she is mostly their primary caregiver. Candice's mom has cancer, and lives over a thousand miles from her. I've known Candice for over twenty-five years and I've worked for her for the last two years. She knows I am serious about my faith and generally I would say she holds me in high regard. I've offered to pray for her, which she appreciates, and she's given financial support for me to go on short-term mission trips.

The other day, while she was telling me about visiting her mom, she broke down crying. I've never seen her cry. As I was sitting across from her, in my head I was trying to bring the gospel to bear on her situation and figure out a way to communicate something of eternal value that didn't sound like I lacked compassion. In the end, I didn't say anything of obvious eternal value. I merely tried to make her comfortable to cry in my presence and to affirm that I had empathy with her situation. I think I could have done better.

As I reflected on that situation later, I wished I had said something like: "This pain you are feeling is normal in a broken, sin-sick world. This world is broken and not like it will be when God reconciles all things to himself." I think I hesitated to say something like that because I didn't want her to assume, like most people do, that there is nothing required on their part

102

to be included in God's reconciliation. Should I have said it any-
way? Should I have said something else?

Kim

These are tough questions in a nitty-gritty world. Here's
how I replied:

Dear Kim,

Well, first off, I think that allowing someone to feel comfortable to cry in your presence is worth quite a bit, but I know
how you feel—it's that sense that we have something so pre-
cious to offer and of such consoling power that in the midst of
heartache, if we could just break through all the defenses that
are set up around people's hearts against Christ, they could
know the one who will one day wipe away all tears. And to
make matters worse, we know how close they are to the truth—
"It's in my heart and I'm right next to you"—but they just can't
see it.

But more to the point about Candice: maybe God is break-
ing down the barriers against Christ in her heart through your
witness. Of course, I'm not sure what the Holy Spirit has in the
works, but it may just be that consoling her was the best thing
to do at the time in a long string of good things she has seen
in you.

The thing to do now, in my mind, is to have a follow-up
conversation. Would it be possible for you to take Candice for
a coffee and conversation? I'd say something like, "Candice,
I want to have a spiritual conversation with you over coffee;
would that offend you?" In my experience, when we reassure
people that we know that faith can be offensive, they tend to
be more open.

Over coffee or a meal, I'd say what you said (I love the way
you put it): "This pain you are feeling is normal in a broken,

sin-sick world." I would certainly encourage you to say that, but then at that point, I would ask permission, again, to tell her how God reconciles a broken world to himself: "Candice, could I have your permission to tell you about how I think a loving God works in the world that's broken?" and then, "Candice, your tears really touched me, and as I've thought about it, I can't think of anything that would be more important to know in your situation than the message of Christ," or "I know that religion can be divisive, but Candice, for the last two thousand years people have found the message of Jesus to be the key to understanding life and death, and I want to tell you about it," or "Candice, you know that I believe in a God on a cross, that is, a God who has identified with our death. And it has such bearing on your situation that I just want to explain the message of Jesus to you"—something like that, or maybe a combination of all those. You would know better how to say it in your context and Candice's, but the goal is to give an honest presentation of the gospel that is full of eternal significance and helps her know her greatest need: to repent of sin and respond in faith.

In one sense, my concerns would be more for her mother to hear a clear gospel presentation if she hasn't before, but I'm getting beyond what you have told me. By the way, you might be helped to read the book *Is God Anti-Gay?* by Sam Allberry.

Your brother,
Mack

This exchange reveals some of the basic principles that I act on in conversations with people about faith. They include:

- Give yourself grace when you share your faith. I've noticed that I often fear evangelism because there are so many ways to go wrong. I can flub the message. I can keep silent when I need to speak. I can say things that later I think were stupid.

But it's good to remind yourself that even your mistakes can help you become a better ambassador.

- Meet people where they are.
- Look for open doors. A culture of evangelism is really helpful here. When church members share about the open doors they have seen around them, other members might hear opportunities with which to get involved.
- Be compassionate and maintain a tender heart toward others. Be careful to remember that you are a sinner. Humility commends the gospel.
- Remember that we have the answers to life's biggest questions. That's something you can offer. When the reality of life pierces through the superficial barriers that keep people from God, that's where you can shine the light of the gospel. Don't hide it under a basket.
- Focus on people's separation from God, not on being morally upright.
- Be intentional in your conversation. Plan out what you will say. This helps you to say things that are helpful, and not say things that are awkward or offensive.
- Acknowledge what we know and what we don't. Kim's phrase, a "sin-sick world," acknowledges the truth we see around us. The Christian does well in that environment because he or she knows how it got that way. I also find it helpful to tell people that I don't always know the whys of what God does, but that I trust him as the one who makes sense in a broken world.
- It's good (though not required) to ask permission to share the message of the gospel.
- Ask lots of questions. Be a good listener.
- Finally, if you anticipate a certain issue in a person's life, it's good to be acquainted with it by reading a book or talking with someone who knows about the issue.

AMBASSADORS MUST BE BOLD AND CLEAR

If I were in jail for evangelism, I'm pretty sure that I would be asking friends to pray that God would "get me out!" But the imprisoned Paul's prayer requests were for boldness and clarity with the gospel (Eph. 6:19; Col. 4:3–4).

It's my sense that boldness is the most needed element for evangelism for the Christian community, at least in North America. This is a place where we can learn well from our brothers and sisters who live where there is no religious liberty.

I first got to know an Iranian named Farshid when he came to our house in Dubai for a student gathering. We sat together while Nisin gave a talk. There were perhaps thirty students in the room. As Nisin talked, I noticed that Farshid was uncomfortable. Finally, he leaned over to me and said, "Mack, he's a great speaker, but when is he going to get to the gospel?"

At last I understood why he was restless. Farshid wanted the gospel to be clear to the students. "Don't worry, brother," I said, "I have never known Nisin to leave out the message of life—it'll come." And it did: Nisin proclaimed the amazing story that Christ saves sinners. As he did, Farshid stopped fidgeting and his eyes filled with tears. I have found that those who come from a background where many hate the cross tend to love it all the more.

The following year, I had lunch with Farshid in Capetown, South Africa, during the Lausanne Congress. He said things were getting hard in Iran and that he sensed it was just a matter of time before he would be arrested—merely for being a bold and clear witness of the gospel. He left the safe fellowship in Capetown for Tehran; what a brave brother.

On Christmas Day, Farshid was arrested; the charge was "treason against the Islamic State of Iran," or, to put it another way, being a faithful witness to Christ. His sentence: six years. His wife and two small children fled over the Turkish mountains to a refugee camp. He's being held in the notorious Evin Prison in Iran. When he is able to slip a letter out of jail, Farshid asks his friends to pray that he would be bold and clear with the gospel, and that he would continue rejoicing in Christ.

Most of us don't face such hardships for being faithful. But Farshid loves Jesus and his gospel. Like Paul, he *counts everything as loss because of the surpassing worth of knowing Christ Jesus* (Phil. 3:8). So he bravely and clearly continues to tell the people around him about the salvation found in Christ.

Take courage from Farshid's story and be bold and clear with the gospel in your own setting. The Bible calls us to remember those who have been brave and faithful, and to follow their example.

AMBASSADORS MUST DELIVER THE MESSAGE AND TRUST CHRIST FOR THE RESPONSE

Four of us gathered at the baggage claim in O'Hare Airport. We had come to Chicago for an important business meeting. In fact, the meeting started long before we got to our hotel: we were deep in discussion as we jumped into the taxi driven by Ibrahim.

As the discussion of various policy implications raged, Ibrahim announced to me, "You know, this world is amazing!"

I glanced at him, trying to keep up with what was being said behind me.

"Allah has created all this," he said with an expansive gesture toward downtown Chicago, a gesture that sent the car swerving into the other lane. I nodded dumbly while harboring a secret desire to be sitting in the back.

"But the amazing thing about Allah is that he keeps records of all that we do."

"Yes, I agree," I said, struggling to break out of my managerial fog. "I'm a Christian, and I believe that God does keep a complete record."

"You know the difference between you and me?" Ibrahim continued. I felt sure this was not a genuine question.

"You believe that Jesus was God," he continued, "and I believe that he was only a prophet." Ibrahim didn't lack for boldness as a Muslim evangelist.

"That's true, too, Ibrahim," I said. This seemed to encourage him, and he began a theological monologue that lasted until we were almost at the hotel.

But at our destination, Ibrahim grew quiet as I filled in the credit card form. Finally, I had a chance to speak: "You know something, Ibrahim? I agree that Muslims and Christians both believe that all sins are recorded, but the Muslim believes sins are weighed against good works, while the Christian believes Jesus offers forgiveness for sin through faith. That's what I think is the biggest difference. That's why I love Jesus: he doesn't weigh our sins against our good deeds; he forgives our sins because he paid for them."

Ibrahim glanced toward the roof of his cab. "Hmm," he

said. Then he helped me get my bags. As he started to drive off, I wondered whether my words had gotten through. Should I have given him a bigger tip? Suddenly, I saw his brake lights go on, and he spun his cab around. "Maybe I did get through!" I thought. "I bet he wants to ask about Jesus—or maybe about forgiveness!" I prepared myself to lead this man to Christ.

But no, I had simply forgotten to get my credit card back. Ibrahim smiled at me as he handed it through the window. I'm glad he was a good, honest Muslim. But as I watched him leave a second time, I again felt that familiar sense of failure about sharing my faith. I wished I had said more about the gospel, or maybe said it in a better way.

But as I thought about it, I realized that what I could have said or should have said was not the issue. What I *did* say was true, and I would trust God to use that—and not just for Ibrahim, but for me, too. He loves me and loves that I took a stab at standing up for the faith. He really doesn't hold my sin—or my failures, or even my awkward attempts—against me. And if he should choose to call Ibrahim to faith, it won't be because I said everything just right, but because of his grace alone.

It took a while to get my mind back on track for the business meeting because I was rejoicing over God's forgiveness and love. The richness of Christ in my life seemed more real because I had shared my faith. I don't know whether speaking to Ibrahim changed him, but it certainly reminded me of what it is all about: life in Jesus is better than a policy meeting. And it reminded me of God's grace in my own life. Did I know I was forgiven before I told Ibrahim? Sure. But to speak of grace to someone who truly believes in righteousness by works drove that grace deeper into my heart. It's not something I know only intellectually. I pray that one day Ibrahim will know this same hope and joy.

It's good for us to remember salvation is a work of the Spirit. We try to be thoughtful, bold, and clear in the way we tell others about the gospel, but God brings the results. We can rest in that knowledge.

AMBASSADORS MUST NOT LOSE HEART

Paul says in 2 Corinthians 4:1, "Therefore, having this ministry by the mercy of God, we do not lose heart." We need to remind ourselves of this when we are tempted to feel that our attempts to evangelize are useless.

While traveling, I ran into Craig in the Cincinnati airport. I knew Craig from church. He identified himself as a non-Christian who was exploring Christianity, but from my distant observation, he appeared to be more interested in the community at church than the faith. It seemed an unusual coincidence to meet up with him, and I invited him to have a seat with me.

Craig looked the part of a classical violinist: his long silver hair stuck out Einsteinlike from the sides of his head, and at that moment he was staring into the distance with a tired, melancholic expression. He told me he had recently lost his mother to a long illness. This confirmed my sense that our meeting wasn't an accident: God was at work in Craig's life, and I prepared myself to talk to him about Jesus. "Who knows," I thought, "maybe this is his time."

I did the things you're supposed to do. I expressed my concern about the death of his mother and inquired about how he was doing. I didn't force the conversation, and I prayed as I listened, sensing that our time had all the marks of a divine encounter. But as I began to probe about Craig's response to Jesus, his guard went up. He was fine, thanks. It was a polite and socially acceptable conversation, but seemingly fruitless on the spiritual level.

As I watched him walk away, I acknowledged to myself that I felt weary, too. I was tired of talking to tired people about a treasure they needed but seemed not to want. I was tired of my silly fears of rejection. But most of all, I was really tired of feeling that I shouldn't feel that way; a feeling that sometimes *made me want to give up sharing my faith.*

Before that tiredness totally overwhelmed me, God graciously guided me to a verse in Philemon that I hadn't noticed before: "I pray that you may be active in sharing your faith, so that you will have a full understanding of every good thing we have in Christ" (Philem. 6, NIV).

Paul has more than evangelism in mind here, but not less. Yet Paul's prayer is for us to be active in sharing our faith. But notice that the reason is neither the response nor our effectiveness. Paul is saying something I rarely hear: that sharing our faith is for our benefit, too, so that we might gain a full understanding of the good things we have in Christ. The Bible says that among all the good reasons to share our faith, one of them is what happens in us. I think this is important not just for us as individual Christians, but for the community as well.

Part of my weariness in evangelism is the constant focus on what is supposed to happen in *others*. When that is my focus and nothing seems to happen, I lose heart. But knowing that God works in me when I actively share my faith gives me hope even when no one responds positively to my efforts.

In fact, I'm convinced that sharing our faith, regardless of the response, is a key to spiritual health for the individual and for the community. Yes, of course we want to be effective in our witness. Yes, many Christians do dumb things that hinder the gospel message—okay, *I've* done dumb things that hinder the gospel—and we should take steps to change those things. But if we want to understand the riches of Jesus more deeply, we still need to share our faith actively.

Craig continued to come to our new church after our meeting in the airport. For months, he sat through God-glorifying testimonies and clear gospel presentations with no apparent response. But one day, the first Sunday I was back in church after a long trip, Craig shocked me by standing up and telling how he'd come to Christ. My heart soared to hear Craig share what God had done in his life.

Many months had gone by, Craig told us, before he'd realized that the testimonies he'd heard weren't dramas. He had actually thought of them as enactments of spiritual events by professional actors. For people to reveal how they had come to understand the gospel in such intimate and profound ways fell outside Craig's experience. But as time progressed, it dawned on Craig that these people were talking about *their* lives.

"Well, here I am," he said, "standing in front of you telling you what happened to bring me to faith. . . . I understand the gospel now." Maybe it's just my imagination, but Craig's voice seemed to have lost the weariness. He seemed different to me: full of life.

As Craig told our church that Sunday morning how he came to understand what Jesus had done for him, I felt my weariness lift, too. I didn't lead Craig to Jesus, but I was active in sharing my faith with him; I had a role. I was a part of a church that had a culture of evangelism. And this time, at least, God let me see how my tiny part played out.

Most of the time, we don't get to see that; we have to trust God. But that's a *good* thing. God is working through us as we share our faith—even if we don't see it this side of heaven. Maybe he works through a bit of time shared in a restaurant lobby; maybe through a brief conversation in which we share the gospel in a minute, or maybe through an important theological observation about forgiveness. Who knows, maybe it's something you will actually do today?

So take hope, even amid discouragement. Know that God is at work through and in you. You can depend on him. Don't be tempted to quit.

After Craig shared his faith story in church, a number of non-Christians went up to him to talk more about Jesus. Craig was shocked by their response. He expected people to think he was crazy. But what he really couldn't get over, he told us later, was the desire in their hearts that only Jesus could meet. "I don't know how you can stand it," he said, "to see that kind of need in people's souls."

I know what he means: sometimes I don't know if I can stand it. In fact, I saw that need in Craig and was tempted to give up. Maybe those tired people around you make you wonder if you can take it. Maybe fruitless attempts to share your faith with a neighbor you see day after day or a taxi driver you see once in a lifetime have made you wonder if it's worth it. Maybe you're secretly tempted to give up, too.

Take heart. Evangelism is bigger than what we see. Remember God's promise: he is giving you a fuller understanding of the good things we have in Christ. He's giving you his eyes to see people as he sees them. He's helping you know the rich meaning of the message we bear, and he's helping you depend upon him to work in people's lives.

Those are enough reasons to keep going, but it gets even better. Sometimes God lets us see tired people transformed into people filled with light. That's a glorious thing, filled with wonder and hope.

APPENDIX

A GOSPEL EXPLANATION

Our Creator God is holy, just, and loving. We are his people, made in his image. Though we were once in fellowship with God and loved by him, we are now cut off from him. That separation of God and his people started with a rebellion by our ancestors. At root, the rebellion was our choice not to believe God and to attempt to make ourselves God instead. That treasonous rebellion failed, and the judgment was eternal death. Horribly, the sin of rebellion is passed on from generation to generation as a curse: all people inherit both the sin and the judgment. Our sin nature makes it impossible for anyone to earn his way back to God.

But even though we are unable to buy or earn our way out of the curse, God in his love provided a way of escape back to a loving, forgiven relationship with him. The entire Bible prophesies, records, and explains the coming of a Savior to do that: God's Son, Jesus.

Jesus, who was fully God and fully man, lived on earth as a miracle worker and teacher of God's ways. He lived a perfect life and became the perfect sacrifice to ransom us from the curse of sin and death. Jesus paid the penalty for our sins through his death on the cross. He rose from the grave, conquering death and proving that what he said was true. Through his death, he purchased the right to offer us forgiveness from sin and the right for any who would turn to him to become children of God.

Anyone who hears this message of good news and responds to Jesus will not be turned away. Jesus calls us to turn from an unbelieving lifestyle and the accompanying sin that ensnares us, and to put our full trust and faith in him alone to rescue us from the curse. So to become a follower of Jesus, we offer our life to him in faith and commit to follow him as Lord for all our days.

DEFINITIONS

- *Evangelism*—Teaching or preaching the gospel with the aim, or intent, to persuade or convert
- *Gospel*—The joyful message from God that leads us to salvation
- *The message from God*—The explanation of who God is, the human predicament of sin and lostness, the work of Christ for our salvation, and the response people must make to gain a restored relationship with God; encapsulated in the four parts of the gospel outline: God, Man, Christ, and Response
- *Sin*—A state of rebellion against God characterized by self-centeredness, unbelief
- *Sins*—The symptoms and expressions of (the state of) rebellion and unbelief
- *Repentance*—Turning from a life of unbelief
- *Conversion*—Moving from death to life, guilt to pardon
- *Belief*—Complete trust in and reliance upon God and his saving grace through Christ

SCRIPTURE PASSAGES FOR THE GOSPEL OUTLINE

There are many Scripture verses you should know about. The following verses provide basic facts about God, Man, Christ, and Response, as well as the cost of following Jesus:

God

- Isaiah 6:1–3. God is holy.
- Colossians 1:16–17; Psalm 8:1–4. God is the Creator.
- John 3:16. God is loving.
- Romans 1:18. God is wrathful toward sin.

Man

- Genesis 1:26–27. We are made in God's image.
- Romans 3:9–12. We all are sinners.
- Ephesians 2:1–3. We are dead in our transgressions.
- Isaiah 53:6. We are in rebellion against God.
- Isaiah 59:2. We are separated from God.
- Romans 6:23. Death is the penalty for our rebellion.

Christ

- John 3:16. Jesus is the way to God.
- Romans 5:6–8. Jesus died for us.
- Romans 6:23. God's gift of eternal life is through Christ.
- Ephesians 2:4–9. God gives grace to us in Christ.
- Colossians 1:19–23. God reconciles us to himself in Christ.
- 1 Peter 2:22. Christ lived a perfect life.
- 1 Corinthians 15:3–4. Christ rose from the dead.
- John 10:10. Christ came to give life.

Response

- Romans 10:9–11. We must confess with our mouths and believe in our hearts.
- Matthew 4:17; Acts 2:38. We must repent.
- John 8:12. We must follow Jesus.
- John 5:24–25. We must hear Jesus's word.
- John 1:12. We must believe in Jesus's name.

Cost

- 1 Peter 1:18–19. Christ redeemed us by his blood.
- Ephesians 2:8–9. God saved us by his grace.
- Luke 9:23–24. We must deny ourselves and take up the cross.

NOTES

Chapter 1: Of Altar Calls and Laser Lights

1. J. I. Packer, *Evangelism and the Sovereignty of God* (Downers Grove, IL: InterVarsity Press, 1979), 48.

2. Tim Keller, *Paul's Letter to the Galatians: Living in Line with the Truth of the Gospel* (New York: Redeemer Presbyterian Church, 2003), 2.

3. The word normally translated as "gospel" in the New Testament is usually translated as "good news" in the Old Testament (e.g., Isa. 52:7).

Chapter 2: A Culture of Evangelism

1. Barna Group, "Evangelism Is Most Effective Among Kids," Oct. 11, 2004. https://www.barna.org/barna-update/article/5-barna -update/196-evangelism-is-most-effective-among-kids#.UjmEo -AXd3g.

Chapter 3: Connecting Church and a Culture of Evangelism

1. The Acts 29 Network is dedicated to planting churches. The name comes from the fact that the New Testament book of Acts has twenty-eight chapters. Therefore, "Acts 29" can be understood as the ongoing "next chapter" in church history. http://en.wikipedia.org /wiki/Acts_29.

2. For more on church membership, see Jonathan Leeman, *Church Membership: How the World Knows Who Represents Jesus* (Wheaton: Crossway, 2012).

3. This book is a part of a series on biblical doctrines and practices that help churches to be healthy rather than sick, to thrive rather than merely survive. We've settled on nine marks on which to specially focus, though many others could be added. The first "mark"

of a healthy church we discuss is the pastor's primary job description: expositional preaching, preaching in which the main point of the biblical text is the main point of the sermon. Sermons that work through books of the Bible should feed into, and lean on, a cohesive understanding of the whole story and message of Scripture. Hence, a second mark is biblical theology. The core message of Scripture, the gospel, is what gives life to our churches, and we must understand it biblically—a third mark. From this flow biblical understandings of conversion and evangelism, marks four and five. Once people are converted, they should be added to the church: hence, church membership. The flipside of membership is discipline, what a church does when members stop repenting of sin. So we're up to seven. Mark eight is a biblical understanding of growth, and the ninth is biblical church leadership.

Chapter 4: Intentional Evangelists in a Culture of Evangelism

1. Donald S. Whitney, *Spiritual Disciplines for the Christian Life* (Colorado Springs: NavPress, 1991), 106.

2. Ibid., 108.

GENERAL INDEX

SCRIPTURE INDEX

Let me hear from you:
mackstiles@gmail.com